The Nightclub Security Manual

A guide for the nightclub security industry

By Tony O Brien

ISBN-13: 978-1723242786

ISBN-10: 1723242780

Contents

Introduction

I have written this manual for several reasons. Firstly, I have worked for almost 18 years in and around the nightclub security industry. Throughout my time working in, training and consulting with nightclubs one of the biggest failures I see is the lack of an operations manual for the security team. Security is one of the key roles in a nightclub and goes a long way to how the entire venue will be perceived by the public. Your security team are the ambassadors of the venue and they should be given the correct guidance on how the venue wants them to look, act and behave towards the public.

The second reason is that as a security employee I would have loved if my employer had come to me and showed me exactly what they expected of me. In general, people in the security industry thrive in well planned, organised environments where they can apply a certain level of control over situations. Having a security manual ensures that everybody is operating with the same knowledge and using the same procedures. This consistency of approach looks and feels more controlled and this has he benefits both for the security team and customers.

Thirdly, having staff who are trained and confident in their role leads to happier and more competent staff. Knowing what to do during the basics gives security staff confidence in performing the basics. Knowledge of what to do an emergency is a starting point for training in emergencies. Once we have a framework for our practice drills they become more focussed and more efficient.

Lastly, the most common reasons I am given by nightclub managers for not having a security operations manual are that they don't have either the expertise or time to compile such a manual and don't have the budget to have a security consultant design one. I'm trying to help them out here by doing most of the work for them. All that a nightclub manager must do now is take this manual and personalise it for their own venue using some or all the material provided.

This manual is not just for nightclub managers though. It's for door supervisors, head door supervisors, security supervisors, security managers and trainers. It can be used just a source of knowledge of good practice by individuals who simply want new information about their role. It can be used by more senior staff to inform their own set of procedures if they don't like the format of mine. It can also be used by trainers to enhance their own programmes and build a security training curriculum for their venue.

I am based in Ireland and most of my work in the night time economy has been here. There are sections in the manual where legislation has been referred to and this legislation is from the Republic of Ireland. Obviously if you are reading this in any other jurisdiction there's a little extra work in it for you to research your own local legislation.

Finally thank you for purchasing my manual. The material collected in here has taken me many years of work and learning to amass and I hope you find it beneficial. I love to get feedback from the industry so if you find of the book useful, not useful, wish to recommend further material or just want to say hello please get in touch. Drop me an e-mail to info@securityoperative.ie with your thoughts.

STAY SAFE OUT THERE

Tony

How to use this manual

This manual is designed to do two things:

1. Give you a lot of great information on good practice to build a complete security training curriculum
2. Help you write your own manual specific to your venue.

You can choose to use it for one, both or neither depending on your position in the industry. Throughout the manual you will see coloured boxes like this:

> **Writers Note:**
>
> These boxes are for those of you who are using the manual to create your own material. In each of these boxes I will give you an overview of what the expected content should be for the section which follows it and provide some areas that you many want to consider when writing your own.

Following each of the coloured boxes will be content which I believe makes up good practice in the area. Don't forget though that the manual you design is yours not mine. I can give you some helpful information and point you in the right direction, but I probably have never been inside your venue. You can use this as a guide but just because I say something in here doesn't mean that it will work in your venue for your customers so bear that in mind. The manual can also be supplemented by the resources and articles on our website www.securityoperative.ie which contains lot of additional thoughts and opinions in the area which may assist you.

The manual is written in 5 sections:

1. The venue
2. The security team
3. Standard operating procedures
4. Emergency procedures
5. Administration issues.

At the back of the manual you will also find a range of appendices containing templates to help you get your security documentation set up to a decent standard.

Section 1: The Venue

Aim of this manual

Writers Note:

This is your opportunity to set out your vision to new and existing employees. Tell them why this manual is in place and how important it is to their role.

Stress the importance of providing a safe and enjoyable experience for both staff and customers but be honest with employees. The procedures contained in the manual are your expectations of your employees and if they fail to meet those expectations then the manual can also be used for both training and disciplinary reasons also.

An assessment following their initial training in these procedures is a good idea. It tells you that not only have you supplied them with the knowledge but that they understood it. A sample assessment is contained in the appendices section.

This manual has been designed as part of ABC Nightclub ongoing commitment to providing a quality security service to its patrons and its employees. It is designed to ensure the consistent provision of an excellent standard of service, an enjoyable place to work and most importantly a place of safety for all occupants of the venue.

The manual has been designed by ABC Nightclub management to cover all the requirements of a security operative working in the venue. It is designed to assist with the training of all security staff who will work in the nightclub and allow them to transfer their skills into their workplace effectively. The manual outlines the staff roles and responsibilities as well as standard operating procedures, emergency actions and other relevant information about working here.

Once you successfully complete this manual and the associated training you will take a simple assessment to ensure that you have retained the required knowledge to begin working in the vital role of security operative. This assessment will be retained on your training record as will all future refresher training records.

The manual with be reviewed annually to ensure that all information within is kept up to date. If you have any feedback for our management on the content of the manual, please let us know. We value the input of our entire team regardless of the length of time in your role and we can only get better together by continuing to evolve as a venue and as a security team.

Introduction to ABC Nightclub

> **Writers Note:**
>
> This section is for a little background on the venue. Some of its history, the crowd profile and the type of entertainment that customers experience. Try to instil a little additional pride in employees by giving a positive impression of the place they will represent.

ABC nightclub opened on Main Street in 1995 and this year celebrates its 22nd anniversary as the city's premier entertainment venue. Comprising 2 separate venues we pride ourselves on providing a diverse range on entertainment for all tastes and ages. The ABC nightclub opens Thursday to Sunday in peak season and on Friday and Saturday nights in the off season. The nightclub opens its doors at 22:30 and plays mainly dance and chart music until late.

The Lounge Bar opens every night and primarily play 70's, 80's and 90's music. During the day, The Lounge Bar serves some of the finest lunch menus in the city and this continues with an evening Lite Bites menu until 21:00 nightly. The Lounge Bar is a laid back and comfortable environment to enjoy drinks before heading to the main nightclub later in the evening. The Lounge Bar stops serving at 00:30 each weeknight and 01:00 at weekends.

Once patrons enter either venue they can move between the two areas freely. At our busiest we have the capacity to entertain over 2000 patrons across all areas.

Organisational Structure

The below organisational structure represents the chain of command within the venue. While most instructions to the security team will come from the Security Manager via the Head Door Supervisor or Internal Supervisor other members of more senior management may from time to time issue requests to carry out specific tasks. Should any person above the Security Manager issue a security team member with a reasonable request it should be carried out and notified to the Security Manager.

In the absence of the Security manager the head Door Supervisor will assume their duties.

Role	Name	Contact	Photograph
Owner		N/A	
General Manager		423567	
Manager 1		423467	
Manager 2		445678	
Security Manager		4232145	
Head Door Supervisor		N/A	
Internal Supervisor		N/A	

Section 2: The Security Team

The Role of Security at ABC Nightclub

> **Writers Note:**
>
> A brief overview of the expected role of the security team. Use this section to set the scene for what the role is and what it represents. Further details will be added in later sections.

The security team are responsible for the safe and smooth operation of all entertainment events at the nightclub. We do this by providing a fully trained professional security team to ensure the safety and enjoyment of patrons and staff. We promote patron satisfaction by communicating in a courteous and professional manner with all concerned to address all of their needs. As a security team member, you are an ambassador for the venue. You are one of our greatest assets in providing safety, security and service to each and every person who walks through our doors. Everything you do including your presentation, behaviour and actions must represent yourself, the security team and the venue in a positive way.

Code of Conduct

The code of conduct set out below is the minimum standard of behaviour for each member of the security team. It is important that you make yourself aware of its contents in detail. We take the conduct of our security team very seriously and our expectation is that this code of conduct is adhered to at all times while representing the venue.

1	Be punctual and attend work in good time. All security team members must be at the venue a minimum of 15 minutes before their designated start time to ensure they are equipped and briefed prior to work beginning.
2	When requested to carry out any task it should be done promptly and in a professional manner. If you are unable to carry out a reasonable request, you must contact your supervisor immediately to notify them of the reason.
3	Do not leave your position unless there is a valid reason to do so. Valid reasons include dealing with a customer issue or responding to a request for assistance. Should you need to leave your position for any other reason you must notify your immediate supervisor and await cover for your location or confirmation to leave from your supervisor.
4	You may from time to time be required to complete reports or statements in relation to your duties at the venue. You must ensure that these statements are true, correct to the best of your knowledge and written in the correct format.
5	All security operatives must make records of all occurrences in the venue in which they are involved. These records include notebook entries, log book entries and a variety of inspection checklists. These documents should be maintained accurately and correctly by all security team members.

6	Maintain confidentiality on any matter relating to the employer, your work colleagues and our patrons. As part of your role you may have access to the personal information of many patrons. You must never breach the privacy of the organisation or its patrons by divulging personal information to third parties.
7	Maintain a very high level of personal integrity, and be scrupulous in accounting for keys, money or property received regarding your role.
8	Extend courtesy to persons encountered during work, ensuring that any exercise of authority is only that required in connection with the venue. We rely on repeat business and we expect you to do your part in ensuring this in all of your dealings with the public.
9	Ensure that any actions taken by them are such as not to bring discredit on the employer, the client or fellow employees.
10	Wear the employer's uniform and use their equipment and identification only with the employer's authority. Uniform should be always neat, clean and ironed and should be in line with the venues uniform and equipment guidelines.
11	Ensure that you are not under the influence of, or consume, alcohol or restricted drugs prior to or whilst at work. Please note that the company will consider this as gross misconduct.

12	Immediately notify any conviction for a criminal or motoring offence to the employer. This includes any cases which may be pending.
13	Not allow unauthorised access to a client's premises. This includes waiving of entry fees or allowing persons entry via a doorway that is not a designated entry point.
14	Ensure that they use employer's equipment or facilities only with authorisation.
15	Not engage in any behaviour or actions that may endanger the health safety or welfare of any other person. This includes yourself, your colleagues, other employees or members of the public.

Breaches of this code of conduct may in certain circumstances be considered gross misconduct and may be subject to disciplinary action up to and including dismissal.

Security Appearance and Equipment

Writers Note:

In this section outline the expected level of uniform, personal appearance and equipment required of the security team. It is important to be as prescriptive as possible to reduce inconsistency in security dress.

Outline the equipment required and which items of that equipment will be supplied by the venue and which will need to be supplied by the security operative themselves. Also detail any personal protective equipment which will be issued to security staff.

In order for our security team to project a confident and professional image to members of the public a high standard of personal appearance is required.

A few points on the security operative's appearance and necessary equipment are outlined below:

- Security operatives are expected to be clean shaven always. Where a beard is worn it must be neatly trimmed.
- No jewellery and/or piercings should be visible while on duty. The only acceptable jewellery to be displayed is a wedding band and a watch.
- Security operatives should wear clean, polished black shoes or boots. These should be durable, waterproof and have good gripping soles. These should not be of the slip-on type for safety reasons. Shoes are required to be supplied by the security operative.
- Clean, ironed black trousers should be worn by security. No jeans combat trousers or tracksuits should be worn. Trousers

should have pockets. Trousers are required to be supplied by the security operative.

- Each security team member will be supplied with 3 shirts containing the company logo. The security operative's shirt should be clean and ironed at all times. Shirts should be long sleeved and proper fitting.

- A strong black belt should be worn on the trousers. Without this a radio or other security equipment cannot be worn. This belt should have a plain buckle on it. This must be supplied by the security operative.

- Security are issued with two clip on ties. The tie must always be worn while on duty. If it is dropped or lost at any time during your shift you must notify your supervisor immediately so that a replacement may be supplied.

- If you are issued with a security jacket you must wear it while on duty. Any lost or damaged jackets must be immediately reported to your supervisor.

- In accordance with current licensing legislation your security licence must be openly displayed while on duty. The venue will supply an armband licence holder, and this must be worn at all times to display your licence.

- During cold weather, it is acceptable to wear a black/navy fleece under your jacket while on external positions.

- It is not acceptable for security operatives to wear hats, caps or other headwear while at work for safety reasons.

- A notebook and pen are essential items of a security operative's equipment and should be carried at all times. The black hardback notebook and pen will be issued to each security operative. Your notebook should be used to record all incidents which occur during your shift. It is essential that your notebook is kept in excellent condition. The notebook should be returned to the security manager once completed and a replacement will be issued.

- It is advised that all security operatives carry a small torch while on duty. The torch has numerous uses including: (1) Getting the attention of other security team members. (2) Checking security features on ID's. (3) Highlighting broken glass and spillages in low light conditions. (4) Searching. (5) First aid situations. A small torch will be issued to all security operatives. This torch may be worn on the belt in the pouch provided. Batteries for the torch are available in the security control room. It is the responsibility of the security operative to ensure that the torch is working prior to each shift.

- All security staff will be issued with a two-way radio at the beginning of their shift. All security operatives will also be issued with their own individual earpiece and microphone unit.

- It is advisable that security operatives wear a wrist watch to work. We do not wish to see security operatives checking mobile phones during their shift, so a watch is advisable to record the times of incidents.

All items of uniform and equipment issued to security officers by ABC Nightclub remain the property of the company. It is the security operative's responsibility to take reasonable steps to prevent any loss or damage to these items of company property. It is also the security operative's responsibility to ensure that they follow these guidelines and ensure they attend work with the correct uniform and equipment. Subject to normal wear and tear the venue will replace security uniforms periodically and replace equipment as required. If the security manager deems that a security operative is being negligent or abusive with uniform or equipment they may be asked to contribute to the cost of replacement above the normal wear and tear period.

Personal Protective Equipment

As part of its ongoing commitment to staff safety and welfare and in accordance with current Health and Safety legislation ABC Nightclub will provide all security team members with personal protective equipment (PPE). The level of PPE required is dependent on the level and nature of the risk involved in your role but may include:

- Hi-Visibility Clothing such as jackets or vests to all team members working in external positions. Hi-visibility clothing may also be issued to internal security staff on busy nights
- Disposable Gloves: All security staff are required to carry disposable nitrile gloves on their person at all times. Gloves are available from the first aid room,
- Hearing protection: All internal security team members are required to wear hearing protection throughout their shift. Ear plugs are available in the security control room. Supervisors will check individual security team members for compliance with this instruction throughout their shift.
- Waterproof clothing: Will be provided to staff members working in external positions where cold or wet weather occurs.

The level of PPE will be decided by the Head of Security after he/she undertakes a risk assessment of the situation on a night by night basis

Prohibited equipment

ABC nightclub prohibit the carriage or use of any illegal items or offensive weapon by members of the security team. This includes:

- A knife or bladed object

- A baton or impact weapon
- A firearm or imitation firearm
- Handcuffs or restraint equipment
- Any item which produces an electrical discharge or sprays any noxious liquid

Any security team member who is found in possession of any of the above or any other item deemed inappropriate will be subject to disciplinary action and the Gardaí may be informed.

Role and responsibilities of the security team

Writers Note:

This is a brief overview of the expected duties of the security team. List format is fine, and these will be expanded upon in later sections.

While the specific responsibilities of each security team member will vary according to their position within the venue and the specific event that night the general responsibilities will remain constant and will include:

- Access control
- Fire Safety
- Health & Safety

- Crowd Safety
- Enforcement of venue policy
- Customer service
- Physical presence
- Monitoring intoxication.
- Monitoring drug use
- Conflict resolution

Duty of Care

Writers Note:

In this section outline the venues expectation of the security team from a legal perspective. Set the expectation that they are not expected to put themselves at excessive levels of danger as part of their role. Emphasise the fact that all actions have consequences and reckless behaviour can be breach of your duty of care.

As a venue ABC Nightclub has duty of care to provide a safe place of work for all of its employees and to maintain a particular standard of safety for all of its patrons while on the premises.

As representatives of ABC Nightclub, the security team members have responsibilities for upholding this duty of care.

Duty of care is best described as taking responsibility for all your actions or omissions while on duty which may result in you or another person suffering an injury or a loss because of them.

You must bear in mind your 3 basic priorities regarding your duty of care while at work:

1st Duty of Care: Your first responsibility is for your own safety. At all times your primary concern is your own personal safety. This means you should take no action which you could reasonably believe may result in an injury or a loss to yourself. You must also not fail to take any reasonable precaution which would have prevented the injury. This could include actions taken deliberately or recklessly.

2nd Duty of Care: Your second responsibility is for the safety of your fellow security team members. Once you are assured of your own personal safety you should endeavour to take all reasonable steps to maintain the safety of your team. You must always remember that your actions could influence the safety of your colleagues.

3rd Duty of Care: Your third responsibility is the safety of the patrons in the venue. Provided it is safe for yourself and the rest of the security team you must take all reasonable steps to ensure the health, safety and welfare of all the patrons within the venue regardless of what their actions have been.

Health and Safety policy

ABC Nightclub regards the safety, health and welfare of its employees with paramount importance.

The company shall at all times endeavour to maintain a safe working environment and conditions for its staff. The company will not request any staff member to take any action which it feels would put the staff member at undue risk of danger, injury or ill health during or associated with their employment.

In accordance with this policy the company shall design a risk assessment and standard operating procedures to provide guidance and training to staff on the subject of safety, health and welfare at work.

Failure to adhere to this policy may result in disciplinary action.

Working Hours

Writers Note:

Simply state the hours of work. This can be difficult to define due to the nature of the role with later start times etc. but give a general idea. Let the employee know that they need to be on the floor at that start time and when they can stand down.

Due to the nature of the role of the security team it may not be possible to specifically define your working hours. Security operatives will be given their shift start and finish time 2 weeks in advance via the security team schedule. However, due to the nature of various events you may be expected to remain in position for some time after your scheduled finish time. The security team will stand down only when the venue is cleared, the debrief is finished and all reports have been completed.

Staff Welfare

Writers Note:

This is often overlooked by employers but essential. You can't complain about the security operative ordering a cordial at a packed bar if they haven't been told otherwise. When it comes to breaks my approach is always to grant a small (10 to 15 minute) water/air break during a shift if operationally possible. Talking about staff welfare is important. Staff who feel looked after are more likely to stay than those who don't.

ABC Nightclub is aware of its duty for the provision of welfare facilities to all security staff whilst on duty. This includes the use of toilet and sanitary facilities, drinking water, rest facilities and first aid provision. During site familiarisation training all new security operatives will be made aware of the location and acceptable usage of all staff welfare provisions.

Toilets: There are no separate employee toilets. Security operatives may use the public bathrooms throughout their shift. Security staff should be aware that at peak times there may be a queue. Under no circumstances may security staff use the disabled persons bathroom in lieu of queuing.

Sanitary: A wash hand basin is provided in the first aid room for use by security staff

Drinking water: Bottles of water are available in both the first aid room and the security control room for security operatives. Please do not bring bottles of water into the public areas or to the front door. Security staff are not to queue at the bar and ask for water or any other product during their shift. No hot liquids are permitted at the front door or at your position throughout your shift.

Rest facilities: Where members of the security team work in excess of 4 hours we will always try to facilitate a 15-minute rest break during their shift. At peak times, this may not always be possible, but we will endeavour to do so wherever possible. Rest breaks may be taken in the security office where security operative may eat and drink. This break will not be deducted from pay. During this break security operatives are required to keep their radios turned on and respond to emergency calls. Breaks will be taken in rotation and no more than 2 staff will be on break at any given time.

Staff support: The venue has employees trained in safeguarding techniques. Should any member of the security team feel they require support or just a conversation about difficulties at work or otherwise they can ask to speak to a safeguarding trained operative at any point. The venue is committed to the wellbeing of all employees and will provide various supports to employees who require emotional or psychological support following any workplace incident. Please speak to the Security Manager or a safeguarding trained employee with any concerns you may have. All conversations are fully confidential. Safeguarding employees are listed nightly on the first responders list and a full list is posted in the security control room.

Section 3: Standard Operating Procedures

This section of the manual will detail the standard operating procedures for the security team. Specific events may require deviation from these procedures but generally speaking this will be our safe standard of operation for the nightclub. This section will include details on:

- Pre-shift briefing
- Pre-opening checks
- Access control policies
- Searching policy and procedures
- Lost and found property procedure
- CCTV policy and procedures
- Security positions
- Communication procedures
- Dealing with patron's behaviour
- Dealing with violent patrons
- Recording of incidents

Security Briefing

Before every shift for the Head of Security will deliver a security briefing to all members of the security team. This briefing will cover topics such as:

- Crowd profile and expected numbers
- Duty of care and safeguarding
- Chain of command and key personnel
- Start/finish times including bar and music finish times
- Areas of responsibilities and positions
- Patrolling duties and planned removals
- First aid and welfare
- Emergency actions (fire and major incident)
- Command and control systems (radios/alarms etc.)
- Venue management requests specific to that night (VIP's) etc.

All members of the security team are encouraged to ask questions, take notes and/or make suggestions during these briefings. It is your responsibility to ask questions at the briefing if you are in any way unsure of your role, responsibilities or actions in an emergency.

Pre-Opening Checks

Writers Note:

A brief list of any pre-opening checks to be completed. It is important to build a habit of checking all of the emergency systems and equipment before opening every night.

In order to ensure the safety and security of all patrons and staff attending the venue the security team will carry out pre-shift safety checks before any patrons are allowed access to the venue. These checks include:

- Fire Exits: Unlocked, unobstructed inside and out, opening freely, light working.
- Fire Extinguishers: Correct type, full, not tampered, serviced, unobstructed.
- First Aid Kits: Available, correct positions, fully stocked, in date.

- Communication Checks: Radio batteries charged, radio checks completed.
- Security Equipment: Hi-vis jackets worn, torches working, UV light working

You may be asked as part of your role to carry out all or part of this check. Where this is requested you must report back your findings to the Head of Security following your inspection along with details of any issues or faults detected. A pre-opening checklist is provided for this and must be completed and returned to the Security Manager each night.

Access control policies and procedures

Writers Note:

Outline all the access control policies and procedures which apply. This can include areas such as the queue set up, dress code, identification policy, refusal policy, house rules etc. Be as specific as possible in this section as it may have to be defended legally later. Regardless of whether the individual staff member being trained is to be positioned in an access control position they must be familiar with all the venues policies and procedures in the area.

ABC Nightclub has a strict access control and admissions policy in order to maintain a safe and enjoyable entertainment environment for all of its patrons. This access control policy is the responsibility of the security team to implement.

It is our intention that all of our staff and patrons are able to enjoy all of the services and facilities we offer in a safe manner and in line with all legislation which applies to the operation of the nightclub. Our staff will facilitate patrons in this respect and at all times provide assistance to patrons.

In line with our access control policy we have devised a set of house rules to clearly outline our expectations to all of our patrons prior to entering the premises. All of our access control policies and house rules are clearly signposted at all entrances to the venue. Failure to adhere to or breaches of any of these policies will result in patrons being refused entry to the venue. Where breaches of our policies occur inside the venue patrons will be refused further service and escorted from the premises by security in a professional and safe manner. Any member of the public who is refused entry and/or removed from the premises for a breach of the house rules can be referred to the sign outside of the premises or to the 'House Rules' section of our website or social media pages.

All actions undertaken under the access control policies and procedures must be fully documented by the security team in the security event log.

Queue system

ABC venue reaches its safe operating capacity on most weekend nights. While we endeavour to reduce wait times for customers we anticipate that there will be queues and slight delays at the entry points due to the volume of patrons wishing to enter. To reduce the impact this has on patrons we have devised queue systems which aims to ensure consistent crowd flow through the access points as well as promoting good customer service.

The security team will set up the queue system 30 minutes before the venue is due to open. On busy nights we may extend this to 60 minutes before the venue opens. The queue system consists of crowd control barriers (CCB's), venue branding, access control policy signage and a rope and stanchion system. The security team on the front door are also responsible for removal and storage of the queue system at the end of the night.

Queue Operation

ABC has two public entrances both of which can be busy throughout the night. The main entrance to the nightclub is via the car park while the rear entrance provides access to the bar area. We use two different queue systems at these entrances due to logistical issues in the respective areas.

Both entrances are sufficiently staffed to ensure that patrons wait time is minimised and that they are safe and comfortable during that wait.

Main Entrance

At the main strange we use a serpentine queue system. This ensures that patrons are grouped together in an orderly way. The queue system is shown below.

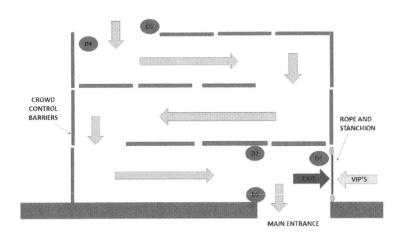

The functions of the security staff on the diagram are as follows:

D1: Head door supervisor: Final decision making on refusal or granting of access, dealing with VIP entrants, liaison with ticket desk regarding capacity.

D2/D3: Access Control checks including ID and patron assessment. Referral of potential refusal of entry issues to head door supervisor

D4/D5: Primary access control filter. Refusal of obviously intoxicated patrons prior to entering the queue. Customer service, removal of alcohol etc. from the queue system. Capacity control in the queue.

Operation of the system

Patrons will enter the queue system and be greeted by security staff at **D4/D5** positions. Patrons will be advised of approximate wait time and asked to leave any alcohol etc at this point.

Patrons will queue to the screening point at **D2/D3**. The security staff will assess patrons and grant access where required. Each patron will be welcomed. If there is a doubt about a patron's suitability for entry they will be referred to the Head Door Supervisor for a decision. Security staff at **D2/D3** DO NOT refuse entry they simply refer the decision to **D1**. Patrons refused entry by the Head Door Supervisor are escorted to the VIP entry point and leave the premises.

At times where the queue has not been occupied to a level where it is fully operational we can make the below alteration to the system.

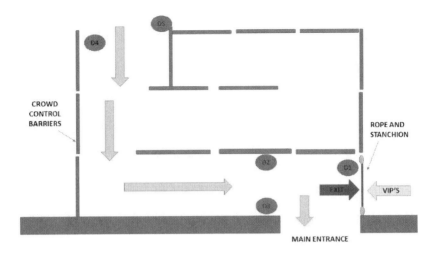

CROWD CONTROL BARRIERS

ROPE AND STANCHION

VIP'S

EXIT

MAIN ENTRANCE

VIP Entrance

VIP patrons who are pre-arranged by the Duty Manager may approach directly to the VIP entrance and be greeted by the Head Door Supervisor.

Rear entrance

Patrons may enter the bar area via the rear entrance and access the nightclub through the venue. The rear entrance is traditionally a quieter entry point however on busy nights a queue can form here. At the rear entrance we use a straight queue system. The queue system is shown below.

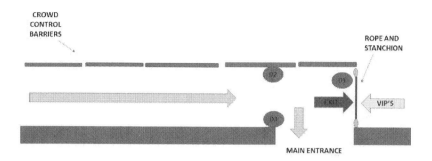

The functions of the security staff at the rear door are as follows:

D1: The Head of Security will appoint a senior member of the security team for this position. This person is responsible for decision making on refusal or granting of access through this area and liaison with ticket desk regarding capacity. For difficult patrons this person will contact the Head Door Supervisor or Head of Security for a final decision on granting or refusing access.

D2/D3: Access Control checks including ID and patron assessment. Referral of potential refusal of entry issues to the person at **D1**.

D4: Customer Service. Removal of alcohol and other prohibited items from the queue.

Operation of the system

Patrons will enter the queue system and proceed to position **D2/D3** for screening. Each patron will be greeted upon entry at **D2/D3**.Patrons will be granted access or referred to **D1** for a decision. Security at

D2/D3 DO NOT refuse access to the venue. They refer all issues to **D1**.

If a queue forms above 50 people a security operative will be summoned from the internal security team to take up position at **D4**. They will establish a queue break of approximately 2 metres after 50 patrons. They will speak to patrons beyond the queue break and inform them of the 5-minute wait time. They will request patrons to have identification ready and to place any alcohol or other items in a bin before proceeding to **D2/D3**.

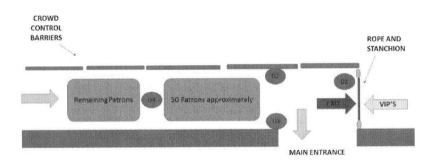

Once all 50 patrons have passed through **D2/D3** the person at **D4** will allow the next 50 people to enter and re-establish the queue break after a further 50 patrons.

House Rules

For the safety and security of our patrons and employees and in accordance with our legal obligations and rights the following house rules apply:

- Strictly over 18's
- ABC reserves the right to use or publish any photos or videos taken on the premises on social media or other media formats.
- As a condition of entry and service in the nightclub ABC reserves the right to carry out random searches on patrons. Refusal to consent to a search will result in refusal of admission or exclusion from the venue.
- Intoxicated patrons will not be granted access to the premises or served further drinks, alcoholic or not, on the premises. Intoxicated persons will be removed from the premises as soon as it is safe and practicable to do so.
- Passport, driving licence, National Age card or European identity cards are the only accepted form of identification. On

specific student nights, we may seek a student ID as a secondary form of identification.

- Neat dress is essential at all times. No hooded jumpers, hats or caps are to be worn on the premises. Items such as these must be taken off while on the premises to enable clear identification of patrons.
- The use of non-prescribed drugs or being under the influence of same while on the premises is strictly prohibited.
- Anti-social or threatening behaviour will not be tolerated.
- There is 24hour CCTV recording in use on the premises.
- The management is not responsible for articles lost or stolen on the premises.
- Management reserves the right to refuse admission
- Footwear must be worn at all times while on the premises.
- Failure to co-operate with a reasonable request from a member of staff may result in exclusion from the premises.
- Soccer jerseys are strictly prohibited.
- Breaches of the house rules will lead to membership of our members and VIP club being revoked.
- ABC nightclub reserves the right to amend these rules at any time. Amendments will be posted on our website and social media pages in advance of any changes and will be highlighted at the entry point a minimum of 7 days in advance of any change.
- Any coats, bags or items of clothing left unattended near or blocking an emergency exit will be removed to the cloakroom.

- Running shoes are strictly forbidden

Legislation

All of our access control policies and procedures including our house rules are in line with various pieces of current legislation including:

- Intoxicating Liquor Act 2003
- Equal Status Act 2000
- Licencing Acts
- Data Protection Act 1998 and 2002
- Heath, Safety and Welfare at Work Act 2005
- Non-Fatal Offences against the person Act 1997
- Occupiers Liability Act 1995
- Misuse of Drugs Acts 1977-2015
- Firearms and Offensive Weapons Act 1990

These pieces of legislation are available in full to be reviewed by the security team in the Legislation folder in the security control room. If a security operative has any queries about any piece of legislation applying to their role within the venue they should direct them to the Security Manager.

Dress Code

The nightclub has a dress code policy which promotes a safe and enjoyable environment free from hazards or potential conflicts in the venue. The policy will be applied fairly and consistently across all

49

patrons and is subject to change only with the approval of the Head of Security.

The dress code includes:

- No running shoes
- No hooded jumpers
- No hats or caps inside the premises
- Footwear to be worn at all times
- No soccer jerseys
- No sunglasses worn inside the premises
- No dirty or soiled clothing
- No torn or ripped clothing

This dress code is referred to in our house rules as neat dress and is published outside the venue, on our website and on our social media channels. Queries regarding the dress code of patrons within the premises should be directed to the internal security supervisor for a decision.

Identification Policy

As a condition of entry ABC Nightclub will only accept a number of government issued identifications as proof of age. These are:

- Full Irish driving licence
- Passport
- National Age Card
- National identity card from another EU member state.

In exceptional circumstances and only with the approval of the Head of Security may one of the following be accepted:

- Student identification bearing the age of the patron
- Work identification bearing the age of a patron
- Public services card
- Private Security Authority licence

As a policy, we ask every patron to produce identification on entry to the premises regardless of appearance or perceived age. Failure to produce identification will result in refusal of admission to the premises.

The only exception to this admission policy is where the patron is personally known to a member of the door security team who will vouch for their age and character at the point of entry.

An A4 poster detailing the security features of each identification is available on the wall in the security control room. All security team members should make themselves aware of the contents of this poster. A Jpeg photograph version of this guide is available from the security manager and can be emailed to any security team member upon request. UV lights are in operation around the entry points and personal UV lights are issued to all door team members for detecting forged or tampered identification.

Possession of a valid form of identification does not guarantee entry to the venue.

Age Restrictions

The age restriction policy is in line with the Intoxicating Liquor Act 2003. Patrons under the age of 18 are strictly forbidden to be on the premises unless at a specific non-alcoholic event for that age group such as a youth disco.

For specific nights or events, we may increase the age limit based on the crowd profile and risk assessment. On these occasions, we will advise customers using signage at the entry points, via our website and via any ticket distribution agencies a minimum of 7 days prior to the event.

Intoxication

Due to the nature of the activities undertaken within the premises there will be instances where intoxicated patrons attempt to gain entry to the premises. Our guidelines on intoxication are clear and are strictly enforced by the security team. Our definition of intoxication is in line with current legislation:

A person who is intoxicated to such an extent as would give rise to a reasonable apprehension that the person might endanger himself or herself or any other person.

Our procedures for dealing with intoxication are that we shall not:

- Admit an intoxicated person

- Serve an intoxicated person

- Give alcohol to another person for an intoxicated person

- Allow an intoxicated person to drink alcohol

- Permit intoxication in the premises

Where a person is found to be intoxicated on the premises our duty of care will apply and that person will be assessed for medical fitness before being escorted professionally and safely from the premises. If the security team feel that there is a safeguarding or wellbeing concern for the patron due to intoxication levels, then our venue safeguarding procedures will be implemented and the patron will be cared for in the first aid/welfare area.

Reasons for refusal

There are a number of legally justified reasons why a patron may be refused entry to the premises including:

- Intoxication
- Identification Issues
- Dress code
- Previous issues with behaviour
- Possession of prohibited items
- Disorderly conduct
- Refusal to comply with any of the house rules

Our policy on the refusal of patrons is in line with the Equal Status Act 2000 Section 15(1) and 15(2) and it is our intention to act at all times in good faith in relation to the refusal of goods or services to any patron. Security operatives will treat all patrons who are refused with professionalism courtesy and respect always.

No patron will be refused under any of the 9 discriminatory grounds as set out in the Equal Status Act 2000:

- Race
- Religion
- Age
- Gender
- Sexual orientation
- Marital status
- Disability
- Membership of the travelling community
- Family status

Where a patron is refused they will be given a valid and legal reason for that refusal. All refusals will be recorded in the control room on the security event log. Where possible refusals will be carried out by the head door supervisor. The table below outlines reasons for refusal and approximate times when re-entry to the venue would be considered.

Reason for Refusal	Approximate time until access allowed
Intoxication	Not within 24 hours
Identification issues	Upon production of a satisfactory identity document (Same night possible)
Dress code	When presented in line with dress code. (Same night possible)
Previous issues with behaviour	At the discretion of the Security manager and/or Head door supervisor but not within 1 week of the original issue

Possession of prohibited items	Alcohol: Upon satisfactory disposal of the alcohol and assessment by head door supervisor. Possession of substances suspected to fall under the Misuse of Drugs Acts 1977-2015: Indefinite. Possession of any offensive weapon as outlined in the Firearms and Offensive Weapons Act 1990: Indefinite
Disorderly conduct	At the discretion of the Security manager and/or Head door supervisor but not within 1 week of the original issue
Refusal to comply with any of the house rules	At the discretion of the Security manager and/or Head door supervisor but not within 1 week of the original issue

Searching Policy

It also however takes up considerable time, resource and intrudes on the privacy of patrons.

If a search policy is required, then ensure it meets the profile of the clientele you are expecting to enter.

Outline the types of search, the procedure to be followed and the safety precautions to be followed for security team members in this section.

Also outline what you expect your security team to do when they find prohibited items during a search.

For the safety of our staff and patrons we have adopted a search policy. Acceptance of our search policy is a condition of entry and continued access to the venue. Our search frequency and type vary from night to night but will be one of three levels:

- **General search policy:** All patrons will be searched at the point of entry.
- **Random Search policy:** Patrons will be searched using a pre-determined pattern.
- **Specific search policy:** Patrons will not be searched on entry, but specific patrons may be selected for individual searches based on previous incidents or suspicious behaviour.

Our search policy is stated at the point of entry and is regarded as a reasonable condition of entry and service on the premises. A patron will be requested to submit to a search at any time either at the point of entry or within the premises. Failure to submit to the search will result in the person being refused entry or being asked to leave the premises.

Searches will be performed by security operatives of the same gender as patrons. We will take all reasonable steps to ensure that a person is over the age of 18 before carrying out a search. Patrons who are selected for a specific search will be escorted to a private room (security office) for this procedure.

The types of search we will carry out include:

- Bag searches
- JOG searches (Jacket and outer garment)
- Body searches

The purpose of a search is to ensure that no prohibited items such as:

- Alcohol not purchased on the premises
- Substances suspected to fall under the Misuse of Drugs Acts 1977-2015
- Weapons or potential weapons

are not taken into or carried by patrons on the premises. Where such items are found we deal with the situation in several ways including:

- Refusal of entry
- Voluntary disposal of goods (alcohol only)
- Arrest and detention for Gardaí where reasonable grounds exist in respect of an arrestable offence.

A recognition guide of common illegal substances can be found in the security control room for reference.

Each case will be dealt with on an individual basis. The Security Manager will be present for all situations where a member of the security team makes an arrest. They will remain with the suspect and the security staff member until Gardaí arrive.

Search procedures

The search procedure varies for each type of search.

- **Bag Search:** The security operative shall request permission to look into the patron's bag. The patron will open the bag and the security operative will look inside. The security operative will not put their hands into the bag. If items need to be removed from the bag the patrons will be requested to do so or will be requested to empty the bag onto the shelf provided.

- **JOG Search:** The security operative shall request the patron's permission to carry out a search. The patron's jacket or other outer garments will then be patted down to identify items which may be concealed within them.

- **Body Search:** For body searches we carry out the SEARCH© procedure;
  - Seek permission
  - Empty pockets

- Assess patrons
- Relay position to patron
- Conduct search
- Hazard analysis

Security operatives who are tasked with carrying out searches will receive specific training in how to correctly carry them out.

Honesty bins will be provided at the search area for the voluntary disposal of alcohol by customers. Security operatives will not confiscate any items of alcohol or suspected illegal substances from any patron. At the end of the night any alcohol disposed of in the honesty bins will be counted, logged in the security event log and disposed of by the security team.

Any items found in the search process aside from alcohol are to be logged immediately in the security event log and followed up with an incident report at the end of shit.

Searching safety precautions

The following safety procedures are to be followed while searching:

- Nitrile gloves must be worn always while searching. A supply of gloves will be available in the area and gloves should be changed regularly and after every find of prohibited items.
- A minimum of 3 security team members will be present in the search area always. This includes 1 male searcher, 1 female searcher and 1 support person/witness in case of any incidents.

- The search area will always be set up behind the access control point (see image below where search team is at position S1/S2). This is to ensure that the person being requested to submit to a search is both over the age of 18 and not too intoxicated to consent to a search.
- Where specific searches take place in the security control room a minimum of 2 security team members of the same gender as the patron will be present.
- Searches will always take place in view of CCTV
- Searches will always be gender specific. Males will search males and females search females. In cases of gender fluidity or transgender patrons the patrons wish will be taken into consideration as well as the wishes of the security operative. This will be treated on a case by case basis.

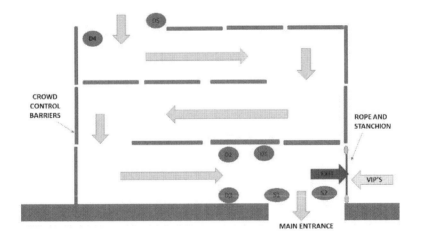

Venue clearance procedure

At the end each night there is a pre-determined venue clearance procedure. The implementation of this procedure ensures that the customers evening ends in an appropriate way and the venue is cleared in a timely manner.

At 5 minutes before the official bar closing time the bar supervisors will dim the lights behind the bars. This will signify the taking of last orders behind the bar. At bar closing time the bar staff will leave the bar area.

The music will stop at bar closing time and the house lights will be turned on by the Duty Manager. Security will remain in position and monitor the crowd for approximately 15 minutes. The Internal Supervisor will then make a radio call to advise all security team members to begin the clearance. A security team member will be appointed by the Internal Supervisor to manage the queue at the cloakroom.

Security will advise all patrons that they have 15 minutes to finish their drinks. They can also advise patrons of the location of taxis and other amenities. Once all patrons have been informed security will return to their positions.

When there is 10 minutes to finish time, security will begin to ask patrons to leave their seats or standing area and begin to move towards the doors. A male and a female security staff member will be deployed to clear and secure the toilets. 2 members of security will get high visibility clothing from the control room and be positioned on the street outside to ensure patrons do not walk on the road and leave the area safely.

As various areas of the venue are cleared a member of security will remain in situ to ensure no re-entry to the area by patrons. The remainder of the team will continue to guide patrons towards the entrance.

The front door security team will remain in position to ensure that no alcohol or glass containers leave the premises. Once the venue is cleared all security will assist in removing and storing the queue barriers and external signage. All security staff will then return to the control room for debriefing and reports.

Lost and found property

Writers Note:

Regardless of the size of your venue you will end up constantly holding onto found property on behalf of your patrons. This is an essential service, however if it isn't manged correctly it can quickly get out of hand.

Security operatives must always be made aware of their duty to protect their own reputation and the reputation of the venue. Holding property (sometimes of value) is a necessary risk and it should be handled and disposed of correctly. It is important to detail exactly what you expect of the security team, when dealing with customer property. You should also detail how property is held, for how long and how it is disposed of at the end of the retention period.

Due to the size and nature of the business undertaken in ABC Nightclub we will inevitably have some patrons who will lose and find articles of property in the venue. Due to the sensitive nature of having to handle other people's property and valuables we have devised a procedure to strictly control the access and management of these articles in a safe and professional way.

In order to reduce our liability for articles lost and or stolen within the venue we had numerous signs throughout the venue stating that ABC Nightclub take no responsibility for items lost or stolen within the venue.

Lost property procedure

Where a patron reports an item of property as lost we follow the below procedure:

- The found property storage area and found property register will be checked to see if the item has been handed in.
- If the item has been handed in, then it will be returned to the patron and an entry made in the found property register to note that the item was collected.

- Where the item has not been handed in then the patrons contact details will be logged along with a description of the lost item. Should the items be handed in at a later date the patron will be contacted, and a suitable collection time will be arranged.
- In the event that a patron disputes or complains about the condition or value of an item which is handed in or collected this will be escalated to the Head of Security to be dealt with through the complaints procedure.

Found property procedure

Where items of found property are discovered or handed in to security then the following procedure shall apply:

- The property will be brought to the cloakroom immediately and stored in the found property area. An entry will be made in the found property register by the cloakroom staff member and countersigned by the security team member.
- Any property left in the found property storage area at the end of the night will be reconciled against the found property log to ensure accuracy. The property will then be removed from the cloakroom to the found property storage area
- The venue will store the found property for a period of 30 days before disposing of the property.

- The found property register will be cross referenced once a week against the lost property register and any property which can be reconciled will be returned to its owner.
- Any purses, handbags, cash, bank cards, wallets or phones found by the security team should be called across the radio immediately on finding and reported as being brought to found property. The security team member will not open bags, purses, wallets etc until arrival at the cloakroom. The contents of the found property along with the value of any cash inside will be logged in the found property register by cloakroom staff and countersigned by security. These items of value will be removed at the end of the night to the manager's office for the retention period.
- Found identification cards, driving licences and passports will be logged in the found property register and removed at the end of the night to the manager's office for storage.

Disposal of property

All property will be retained for a period of 30 days from the date of finding. On a weekly basis the Head of Security and nominated members of the security team will dispose of the unclaimed property which has gone past the retention date. Property will be disposed of in the following way:

- Coats, jackets, bags and clothing will be placed in bags and donated to a local nominated charity.

- Clothing, coats and jackets not in a suitable condition for donation will be torn up and disposed of in the general waste.
- Passports, driving licences and identification cards will be delivered to the local Garda station
- Credit, debit and other cards containing patron names will be cut in half and disposed in general waste.
- Cash will be inserted into the till using a sundry code and receipt attached to the found property register. At the end of the year a donation to charity will be made for the total amount in the sundry code.
- Mobile phones will have the sim cards removed and destroyed. The phones will be donated to a local charity.

All property disposed of will be signed off by the Security Manager in the found property register.

CCTV Policy and procedure

Writers Note:

CCTV is a fantastic tool to assist security teams in nightclubs but also it also carries a significant amount of risk in terms of customer privacy rights.

It is important to detail exactly what CCTV you use as part of your system. What you use that CCTV for, who can access it and for what purpose.

A CCTV risk assessment should be carried out in conjunction with the CCTV policy.

If you are using body worn CCTV this is essential, and you will also need to provide a data privacy impact assessment to keep in line with new data protection legislation. A strict set of operating guidelines should be laid out in your operations manual for the security team members who must use the equipment.

ABC Nightclub operates a 24-hour CCTV recording system. The system is based in the CCTV control room and monitors the entire venue. In keeping with current data protection legislation, we display signage at our entrance which advises our patrons of the use of CCTV recording and the purposes for which this data is collected. The signage states:

"VIDEO AND AUDIO RECORDING IN USE"

"ABC Nightclub operates a 24- hour CCTV recording system for the safety of our staff and customers and for crime prevention. This includes both fixed and mobile CCTV systems which record both video and audio data.

The data will be stored on our secured servers and will be retained for a period of 28 days unless otherwise required to be retained.

The data controller is John Murphy (General Manager) of ABC Nightclub Ltd, who can be contacted at 01 1234567 or info@ABCnightclub.com

All access and other requests regarding your personal data can be made through the number or email address above

The CCTV system

Our CCTV system is located in our security control room. It is a multi-screen digital recording (DVR) system which records a range of static pedestal, static dome and PTZ cameras throughout the venue.

All of our CCTV recordings are securely held on DVR's for 28 days in line with current data protection legislation. In certain circumstances the CCTV recordings of specific incidents may be retained for longer periods. These circumstances include:

- Evidence of a crime
- Incidents where a potential insurance claim may arise
- Breaches of health and safety legislation
- Gross misconduct by employees which may constitute a criminal offence.

Access to the CCTV system is strictly controlled by the Head of Security and will only be granted where there is a valid reason for doing so. Under no circumstances can any member of the security team burn CD's, download to USB or use any other form of recording media to remove CCTV images from the premises. To do so is a breach of data protection legislation and may constitute gross misconduct.

Patrons who wish to gain access or copies of their personal images may request said images in writing to the Head of Security in line with data protection guidelines. Where such a request is made the Head of Security will decide on a case by case basis bearing in mind a number of factors such as; the reason for the request, the type of images and the privacy of other patrons contained in the footage. Patrons who request access to their data should be directed to the Security manager who will assist them in filling in a 'Subject Access Request Form'

Location of CCTV cameras

Our CCTV system is spread throughout the venue and covers most public areas of the club. During initial training all security staff will be given a full tour of the venue including the location and coverage of all CCTV cameras. Where possible security staff should attempt to conduct all interactions with members of the camera in areas where there is full CCTV coverage. This is in order to maximise the safety of the security team member and to protect him/her from claims of improper behaviour or conduct.

A map of the entire CCTV system and its coverage is located on the wall of the security control room. The numbers of individual cameras are printed on this map and are to be referred to in incident reports. A full CCTV risk assessment has been undertaken on the system and is available in the security control room. This risk assessment details each camera, its location and its purpose as well as any privacy concerns associated with the camera or its location. Security team members are advised to make themselves aware of this risk assessment and its content.

Mobile CCTV Units

ABC Nightclub also utilise a number of mobile CCTV units to record patron's behaviour and specific high-risk incidents and situations. Where incidents of violence occur the mobile CCTV, operator will respond and monitor the incident from a distance whilst recording the behaviour and actions of the patron(s) in question. The mobile CCTV operator should not become involved in the incident physically unless the level of risk to themselves or their colleagues requires it.

Mobile CCTV records both video and audio data and as such is subject to strict controls. The data recorded on the mobile CCTV unit will be treated in the same manner as all other CCTV data and will only be used, held or processed in line with data protection legislation. The CCTV recording shall be downloaded to a secure system as soon as possible after each night's operation and access to the storage will be strictly controlled by the Head of Security. The CCTV unit must not be removed from the premises under any circumstances. Where the mobile CCTV unit is used to record specific incidents the footage from these incidents will be retained for as long as is reasonably required for evidence purposes. All other footage shall be deleted after 28 days in line with data protection legislation. The mobile CCTV operator must be aware of the sensitivity of the data in their possession and the improper use of the equipment. Mobile CCTV units should never be worn into bathrooms unless responding to a notified incident of violence or crime.

Staff Operating Procedure for the Use of Body Warn Video

Start of duty

- Staff will recover a camera unit from the equipment room at the start of your shift.
- Each camera is allocated to an individual security team member.

Note: Under no circumstances should a camera be in the possession of a security operative outside of your operating hours.

During duty

During the course of your normal duties, the device remains in a "standby" mode and does not record any material. In order to record an incident, you must deliberately activate the device and, where practicable, make a verbal announcement to indicate that the camera equipment has been activated. This announcement should be present on the recording and if possible, should include:

- The date, time and location;
- The nature of the situation to which the user is present; and
- Confirmation to those present that the incident is now being recorded using both video and audio.

- It also advisable where practicable to activate the unit before making a radio call for support so that the radio call is also recorded on the unit.

If the recording has commenced prior to your arrival at the scene, for example coming to the assistance of another colleague the colleague should, as soon as is practicable, announce to those persons present that recording is taking place and that their actions and words are being recorded. Announcements should be made using plain English that can be easily understood by those present.

At the conclusion of any incident, the record mode on the device is switched off and the captured information is stored.

Unless specific circumstances dictate otherwise, recording must continue uninterrupted from the moment it starts until the conclusion of the incident or the resumption of general patrolling.

The recording is also likely to continue for a short period after the incident to clearly demonstrate to any subsequent viewer that the situation has concluded and that the user has resumed other duties or activities.

Where practicable, users should make an announcement that the recording is about to finish. Prior to concluding recording, where possible, the user should make a verbal announcement to indicate the reason for ending the recording. This should state:

- The date, time and location;
- The reason for concluding the recording.

End of duty

1. At the end of a period of duty, you will return the device to base.

2. Return the camera device to its cradle.

3. You will inform your supervisor if there is any content requiring review.

Camera Usage guidelines

Body Worn Video (BWV) may be used to record video and audio information of encounters between security staff and the public, after ensuring appropriate safeguards in respect of the necessity, legitimacy and legality are addressed in respect of the following:

- prevention and detection of crime
- reduction in incidences of public disorder
- presentation of evidence to Gardaí to bring successful prosecutions before the courts
- transparency of ABC Nightclub practices.
- resolution of complaints
- assist security staff in carrying out their legal duties in relation to licencing legislation
- enable action to be taken in relation to specific incidents
- enable the ABC Nightclub management to deal with complaints
- protect staff as required by the Health and Safety at Work Act 1989 and 2005 while they carry out their duties by acting as a deterrent

Based on the above, the following categories of members of the public are likely to have their contact with security staff recorded:

- witnesses of lawful activities
- witnesses of crimes, or those who witness other parties verbally abusing security staff as they discharge their duties
- witnesses of those who interfere with ABC Nightclub assets including signs and notices
- persons suspected of committing offences

In addition, persons, unrelated to any specific interaction between security staff and any of the categories of persons above, might find their activities captured on a BWV device.

Staff should make every effort to avoid extraneous capture of unrelated persons in video footage.

Mobile CCTV will not be routinely recording and monitoring all activity.

To do so would fundamentally breach the privacy of large numbers of members of the public, who are going about their private business, as well as to a degree the privacy of ABC staff going about their work. This cannot be justified from the perspective of proportionality and legitimacy.

CCTV Data Flow

The chart below illustrates the processes described above and indicates the retention periods for the different categories of footage.

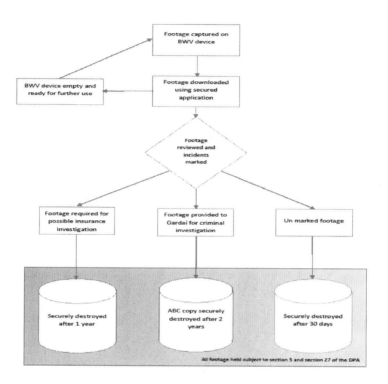

Security Positions

While new members of staff may only be working in specific positions at the beginning of their employment they should at the very least have an awareness of what happens in other positions. As they progress through employment this section forms the basis for their training in each posting right up to the Security Manager who should be able to work in any position and know the protocols for each.

The ABC Nightclub security team will be positioned each night by the Security Manager in line with the type and level of event taking place that night. Security team positions are flexible and security staff may need to be repositioned throughout the night in line with operational requirements. No security team member is guaranteed to work in a particular position and positions will be allocated fairly and in line with the operational requirements on a given night.

Security positions are generally broken into 4 specific areas:

- Access control positions
- Static monitoring positions
- Patrol positions
- Command and control positions

Access control positions

Access control positions are located throughout the venue and are usually located close to the perimeter of the venue. These positions are primarily responsible for controlling patron access to various areas of the club through various access control methods such as ID checks, intoxication assessment, crowd profiling and searching. Access control positions in the venue include:

- **Main door:** The main door is the primary access control point to the club where the majority of patrons will enter through. When the main door is opened it will be staffed by a minimum of 4 staff members. This includes the head Door Supervisor, 2x access control staff and a support/rotation security staff member. The security staff positioned here are responsible for:

  1. Monitoring all patrons entering the venue
  2. Vetting the age of all patrons prior to entry
  3. Observing behaviour and levels of intoxication
  4. Observing for patrons with previous security issues and breaches of the house rules.
  5. Refusal of entry to patrons who do not meet the entry criteria
  6. Referral of individual patron issues to the head door supervisor
  7. Liaising with the ticket desk to control venue capacity
  8. Monitoring patrons who have been refused entry or removed from the venue
  9. Enforcing the venue dress code

10. Communicating incidents of patron's refusals and removals to the other access control points and the control room.

- **Rear door:** This is the secondary access control point for the venue. On nights when this position is open it will be staffed by a minimum of 2 security team members who report to the head door supervisor. The security staff positioned here are responsible for all of the same requirements as the main door above. In addition to the duties outlined above they must also:
    1. Monitor the fire exit door to the right of the position and ensure it is not used to gain access to the venue.
    2. Monitor the smoking area wall to the left of the position to ensure it is not used to gain access to the venue.

- **Search teams:** The search teams are located behind the access control positions at both the main and rear doors. The search teams are made up of a male and a female security team member at each location. They report to the head door supervisor. They are responsible for:
    1. Implementing the search policy of the venue prior to patrons gaining entry.
    2. Liaising with the door security teams around issues found during searches
    3. Ensuring a consistent crowd flow through the search area.

4. Managing the disposal of any alcohol found and handed over by patrons

5. Ensuring a clean and safe search area.

- **Ticket control:** There is a ticket desk inside each entrance which will have a cashier processing the entrance fee. Next to each ticket desk there will be a member of security. The ticket desk positions report to the head door supervisor. The members of the security team who are positioned at the various ticket desks responsible for:

  1. Ensuring that all patrons who enter the venue pay the required charge

  2. Ensuring that patrons behave in a civil manner towards the ticket desk staff.

  3. Provide a degree of physical presence to support ticket operators and the cash desks.

  4. Monitor the level of cash in the desk and liaise with bar management

  5. Liaise with the door teams around capacity issues

  6. Notify the door teams of any removals by internal security staff passing their location

  7. Assist in situations where a single security staff member is escorting a patron past their location.

  8. Keep the ticket desk area clear and free of congestion

  9. Escort the ticket desk operators and cash floats to/from the office where required.

- **Queue management:** For certain events where it is known that a large number of patrons will be queueing early for entrance to the venue we will deploy a queue management team. In instances such as this the security team will set up barriers to form an orderly and safe queueing system to gain entry to the venue. The queue management team will report to the head door supervisor. The security team members in these positions are responsible for:

  1. Ensuring the safety of patrons while queueing and monitoring their behaviour.
  2. Relay any issues with patrons in the queue to the security staff at the main door.
  3. Deny entry to the queue to any patron who is obviously intoxicated
  4. Provide physical breaks in the queue to manage crowd flow where required.
  5. Meet and greet patrons as they await entry.
  6. Remove alcohol containers from patrons before they approach the access control positions
  7. Advise patrons as to the entry criteria while they are queueing.

Static and patrol positions

There are a number of static and patrol positions throughout the internal areas of the venue. The security staff in these positions are deployed in a monitoring and response capacity to ensure the safety and security of patrons within the venue. The internal staff members in these positions are responsible for customer care issues, enforcement of venue policies, monitoring intoxication levels and responding to incidents of conflict and violence. Internal positions include:

- **Bar 1:** This is a static position and reports to the internal security supervisor. The security staff in this position is responsible for:
    1. Monitoring the patrons in their area of responsibility.
    2. Monitor patrons level of intoxication
    3. Enforce internal policies such as footwear and dress code.
    4. Where violent incidents occur, they should liaise with other security team members and manage the situation professionally and safely.
    5. Observe the fire exit to the left of their position and ensure that it does not become congested, blocked or used as an access/egress point except in an emergency.

- **Bar 2:** This is a static position and reports to the internal security supervisor. The security staff in this position is responsible for:
    1. Monitoring the patrons in their area of responsibility.
    2. Monitor patron behaviour and intoxication
    3. Enforce internal policies such as footwear and dress code.
    4. Where violent incidents occur, they should liaise with other security team members and manage the situation professionally and safely.
    5. Observe the bar area for congestion and support the bar staff in keeping the service area clear.
    6. Identify and resolve any potential safety issues in the area.

- **Stage:** This is a static position and reports to the internal security supervisor. The security staff in this position is responsible for:
    1. Monitoring the patrons in their area of responsibility.
    2. Monitor patron behaviour and intoxication
    3. Enforce internal policies such as footwear and dress code.
    4. Where violent incidents occur, they should liaise with other security team member in the stage area and manage the situation professionally and safely.

5. They should be aware of patrons gaining access to the stage.
6. Take routine patrols into the bathrooms to check for issues.
7. Identify and resolve any potential safety issues in the area.
8. Support the DJ or band members with any safety issues they may have.

- **Dance floor:** This is a static position and reports to the internal security supervisor. The security staff in this position are responsible for:
  1. Monitoring the patrons in their area of responsibility.
  2. Monitor patron behaviour and intoxication
  3. Enforce internal policies such as footwear and dress code.
  4. Where violent incidents occur, they should liaise with other security team members on the dance floor and manage the situation professionally and safely.
  5. They are also responsible for ensuring that no drinks are taken onto the dance floor area in line with the venue policy.

- **Internal Patrol:** The internal patrol is a floating member(s) of the security team. If this person is not the internal supervisor, then they will report to the internal supervisor. This person is responsible for

1. Monitoring, supervising, and co-ordinating all the members of the security team working internally.
2. They will have regular check-ins with each position and ensure that they are available to respond to requests for assistance.
3. The person in this position will ordinarily also be a trained first aider who can respond to accidents and injuries within the venue.

Writers Note:

Continue with each internal position as required. Complete a section for each position even if that position is only required on occasional nights. The positions I have used are fictional but give an example of the type of the positions and descriptions that I would advise.

Command and control positions

There are a number of command and control positions within the venue whose role it is to provide leadership, structure, guidance and control to the security team. These positions include:

- **Head of Security/Security Manager:** The Head of Security is responsible for the overall smooth operational running of the security function. They will liaise closely with management on all issues of security, safety and crowd management and will be primary representative of the security team at the venue. Their duties include taking responsibility for the pre-event briefing and pre-opening checks. They will also position each member of security staff as per the security plan and manage any positional or operational changes throughout the night.

The position carries with it the responsibility of representing the company towards both the public and the security staff. They will also take responsibility for the safe keeping and deployment of all company equipment and become the chief point of contact for authorised bodies and emergency services in the event of an emergency incident.

- **Control room operator:** The security control room operator is an integral part of the security team at the venue. The controller provides a liaison between the internal and external teams and the event supervisor. They will have access to the venue CCTV system and they will monitor the cameras and guide the security team to deal with potential events and active incidents. The controller is responsible for the issue and return of all radios and equipment. They must monitor and oversee the radio traffic and ensure a smooth and concise flow of communication across the network. They are also responsible for accurately recording and reporting all incidents both routine and emergency and co-ordinating the security team in the event of an emergency.

Radio Communication

The security team are equipped with a set of analogue/digital Motorola two-way radios. These radios are privately licenced through the Commission for Communications Regulator who have assigned a private bandwidth to ABC nightclub. This means that our radio communications are relatively secure and free of interference. While our bandwidth is private this does not mean that members of the public cannot gain access to our communications.

Equipment Overview

The image below shows the Motorola SL300 two-way radio model used in ABC nightclub. Ensure you familiarise yourself with the location and function of each button from the table below.

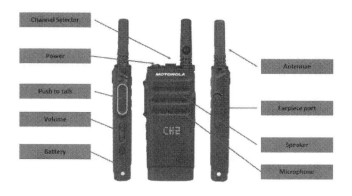

Earpieces

Every security staff member will be issued with their own personal earpiece for the Motorola radio at the start of their employment. The earpieces are the clear acoustic tube type in the image below. If you have not used an earpiece of this type before or are unfamiliar with its fitting or operation, please ask a member of senior staff for guidance. We emphasise consistency in all our security operations so please only use the earpiece we supply you with and do not bring any other personal earpieces to work with you. The only exception to this is where you require a different fitting for medical reasons.

You can cut the acoustic tube to the suitable fitting length but do not make any other alterations or modifications to the equipment. Subject to normal wear and tear and loss or damage during your duties we will replace your earpiece as required. We operate a no blame policy for lost or damaged equipment so please report any loss or damage immediately.

Radio sign out

The two-way radios are stored in the security control room. They will be stored in a charging bay on the desk. Please only remove radios which are showing a green charging LED on the charging bay and the unit. All two-way radios are labelled with the venue name and a number. When you select your two-way radio please sign the 'Radio Sign Out Log' which is located next to the charging bay. Please record the radio number, time out and your name on the log. At the end of the night please return your radio to the charging bay and record the time and your signature. If there are any issues with the radio, please record this in the maintenance issues column of the log.

As with the earpieces we operate a no blame policy for the loss or damage to any radio during your duty. If a radio is lost, stolen, damaged or has any other operational issue please report immediately to the control room and you will be issued with a replacement.

The following rules must be adhered to with regards to all radio communications.

- Ensure you know how to correctly operate the radio assigned to you.
- Ensure you put your radio on charge each night after use.
- Perform a radio check with control on receipt of your radio.
- If using an earpiece, ensure it is firmly attached before turning the radio on.
- Ensure you memorise all the emergency codes in use.
- Keep all conversations brief and to the point. (Think before you talk.)
- Never use bad language on the radio. It is a criminal offence. All radio traffic is monitored randomly by the Director of Communication who can track and fine radio users.
- Never use radios for non-work conversations.
- Remember that even though you are operating on a secure frequency there is always the possibility that somebody is listening in.
- If your radio fails, ensure you inform control ASAP.

- Radios are location specific. Please do not bring your radio off the premises.

- Listen on the air before you transmit to avoid interrupting or cutting off other units.

- Use your call sign to identify yourself before each transmission and wait for control to acknowledge before you proceed.

- Learn the standardised pro-word codes used for all radio transmissions.

- Learn the phonetic alphabet. Read back numbers and letters to confirm accuracy.

- Do not shout into the radio. Speak in your normal voice.

- Hold the PTT (Push to Talk) button for 1-2 seconds to establish a contact before speaking.

- End each transmission with 'over' and end the final transmission with 'out'.

- Never transmit your name or place of work over the radio. Especially when announcing breaks or off duty times.

- Do not transmit any person's personal details over the radio. This includes names, addresses or dates of birth. This is a breach of privacy and data protection legislation.

Radio call signs

Radio call signs are unique identifiers used to identify callers on the radio network. ABC Nightclub use a set of call signs which relate your location within the venue. The position allocated to each individual security team member on a given night will become their call sign. A call sign should be used before broadcast at the beginning of every message to clearly identify yourself on the radio network and so that other security team members can accurately respond to your request. In addition to the positional call signs the below will also apply:

Personnel	Call sign
Venue duty manager	Zero Alpha
Head of Security	Zero Bravo
Head door supervisor	Zero Charlie
Internal Supervisor	Zero Delta
Internal Patrol	Zero Echo
First aid staff	Medic 1, Medic2, Medic 3

Pro Words for Radios

Pro words are a universal radio language used throughout the security industry in order to standardise radio communications and keep all messages as brief, concise and to the point as possible. We use pro-words at the venue to ensure all our communications are consistent and professional. Several regularly used pro words are listed below and all security operatives should be familiar with these phrases and their usage:

Pro Word	Meaning
Stand By	Remain silent and in position to receive further information.
Ignore Last	Last transmission was in error. Please disregard.
Figures	Numbers to follow
I repeat	I am repeating my last transmission
I spell	I will spell phonetically

I confirm/ Please Confirm	I am confirming/please confirm that the last transmission was correct
Over	End of my transmission, I expect a reply.
Out	End of my transmission, I do not expect a reply.
Go Ahead	Ready and waiting to receive your message
Relay to	Please pass this message to
Roger	I have received and understood your message
Time	Time to follow (24 hr clock)
Location	My location is/What is your location.
ETA	Estimate Time of Arrival
Radio Check	Confirm that your radio is working.
RTC/RTB	Return to Control/Base

Phonetic Alphabet

The phonetic alphabet is a coded system for transmitting key words and phrase accurately over the radio. Where an important word or phrase is to be transmitted over the radio is should be spoken first and then spelled phonetically to ensure that it has been transmitted and received correctly. All security operatives should be familiar with the phonetic alphabet listed below:

A	Alpha	N	November
B	Bravo	O	Oscar
C	Charlie	P	Papa
D	Delta	Q	Quebec
E	Echo	R	Romeo
F	Foxtrot	S	Sierra
G	Golf	T	Tango
H	Hotel	U	Uniform
I	India	V	Victor
J	Juliet	W	Whiskey
K	Kilo	X	X-ray
L	Lima	Y	Yankee
M	Mike	Z	Zulu

Sending and receiving radio calls

Our radio procedure format must be used for all standard radio communications. This format is used so that all of our radio calls are consistent, and it is clear to all who is calling and who the message is for. The following format is to be used for all messages:

"(Call sign) to (Receivers call sign) – (message) - (finishing pro-word)"

Example

(Front Door) to (Control)- (Radio check) – (over)

Emergency Codes

Emergency codes are used as a concise method of transmitting an important message or request for assistance. These codes are keep communications within the security team clear and understandable. All security staff should know the emergency codes in use.

Emergency code	Meaning
Code Green	I require another member of security to my location.
Code Red	I require all available members of the security team to my location
Code Orange	Stand by for emergency evacuation
Code Black	Emergency evacuation signal

In the event of an emergency call (Code Red, Orange or Black) you do not need to use call signs prior to sending your message as per the standard procedure above. For example, a radio call for a large violent disturbance on the dance floor would be

"CODE RED, DANCEFLOOR"

Recording of radio communications

Radio communications will be monitored throughout every shift by the security control room operator and recorded on the communications log. This log will be maintained in the security control room for a period of up to 2 years. Security team members will only be identified by their call sign on the communications log and names will never be recorded. Communications recordings are retained to investigate incidents which may come to light many months after they happen and may not have been subject to a report at the time. Any security team member can request to view the communications log for a period of 4 weeks after the time of recording. Any security team member can also request to have an entry to the communications log amended if you feel it is incorrect. You may request a viewing or an amendment via the Head of Security at any time.

Interacting with Patrons

Writers Note:

This heading is a critical part of your manual. The most common complaints you will have about your security team will be around their behaviour when asking patrons to leave, removing patrons or dealing with incidents of violence. In this section it is important to be clear exactly what your expectations are from your security team when interacting with patrons.

Consider how you would like them to greet patrons, how they should deal with complaints, the way in which they ask patrons to leave and how they will manage incidents of violence.

Having a standard procedure for when patrons are asked to leave or when security staff need to respond to acts of violence is important. It makes it clear to everybody what is expected and ensures that the entire team is working from the same page.

Through our professional approach to customer service the clear majority of security operative's interaction with patrons will end satisfactorily for both parties. However due to the nature of the service provided by the security team it will from time to time require our security team manage the risk of disorderly customers. It is essential for both the security operatives' safety and for the image of both the company and the venue that these instances are dealt with in a professional manner.

Patron greeting

When working at any of the access points we expect that the security team greet each guest as they enter and leave where practical. Where appropriate the patron can be addressed by name. The greeting is only where appropriate and does not take precedence over any other security duties.

Complaints

If a patron raises an issue or complaint that the security operative can resolves themselves, they should do so. This is only in relation to security or safety related incidents. Once the complaint or issue has been resolved it should be reported to the control room on the radio to be recorded on the security event log.

If the complaint relates to a service issue (bar or floor) then the complaint should be escalated to the duty manager to be resolved. The duty manager should be called to your location on the radio. The security staff member should remain with the patron until the duty manager arrives.

If a security issue cannot be resolved by the security operative, they should call the internal supervisor or the Head of Security to their location. The security team member may apologise on behalf of the venue when dealing with minor issues but must not admit any liability on behalf of the venue in respect of any issue or complaint.

Requesting a patron to leave

Occasionally it may be necessary for a member of the security team to request a person to leave. This may happen for several reason such as; disorderly conduct, intoxication or venue management requests. We place a considerable amount of trust in you as a member of our security team to act with professionalism and integrity in such situations. We do not ask that you seek permission or authorisation before requesting a patron to leave. We have employed you as a security professional and we trust that if in your professional judgement a person is required to leave then this is the correct decision. While we do not expect you to ask permission we also accept that there are sometimes difficult decisions to be made. If you are in any way unsure as to whether a person should be asked to leave you can request guidance or assistance at any time from any senior member of the security team.

For the security team to deliver a quality security service and to prevent further legal repercussions it is essential that these occasions are dealt with professionally and consistently.

A few points to note:

- We are happy for security operatives to have informal conversations or issue verbal warnings to customers about their behaviour without the need to record this with control or request assistance. This option can be taken at the discretion of the security operative where they feel the behaviour does not warrant the patron being asked to leave. The warning option can be used as many times as a security operative deems appropriate.

- Only a security team member should ask a person to leave the premises. Bar staff, floor staff or cleaners cannot ask a patron to leave or issue a warning. They also cannot request you to remove a patron. The only person who may request you to remove a patron is a duty manager.

- If a duty manager requests, you to remove a patron this should logged using a radio call to control prior to taking any action.

- The only occasion in which a security operative should request a person to leave will be when you believe it meets the legal criteria for doing so

- At all times a witness (security team member) should be present when a patron is asked to leave if possible. We do not condone the use of single person removals unless in an emergency. Even if the patron voluntarily leaves we will have two members of security in the vicinity.

- If you feel a patron needs to leave the following steps should be taken:
  1. Turn on your mobile CCTV unit if you are wearing one.

2. Call a Code Green to your location on your two-way radio
3. The internal supervisor/patrol or the nearest member of available security staff will respond.
4. The control room will also begin to monitor your situation on CCTV at this stage.
5. When your assistance arrives brief them on the situation and decide on lead and support roles.
6. Engage the patron and ask them to leave.

- Where female patrons are asked to leave we require a minimum of 1 female member of security to be present unless in an emergency. When requesting a female patron to leave the female security staff member will take the lead in the removal and speak to the patron. This is opposite if a male patron is required to leave.

- If you are a male member of staff and you require a female patron to leave you should use the radio call "(CALL SIGN) CODE GREEN FEMALE OVER"

- If during an informal conversation or issuing a warning it becomes apparent that the patron needs to be removed, you should step back and begin the steps outlined above for removing a patron.

- To ensure staff safety and consistency of service we employ the REACT method when asking a patron to leave.

R.E.A.C.T.

A person who is asked to leave the venue and refuses will be treated as a trespasser in law. This status means that if the person refuses to leave of their own free will the security team may escort them from the premises. In circumstances such as this the security team may use reasonable force to end the trespass or to prevent an ongoing breach of the peace or criminal act. In every situation the security team will endeavour to negotiate verbally and gain the compliance of the patron. However, it is vital that whatever action is taken it is completed professionally, safely and legally using the below method:

- **R:** Request that the person leaves.
- **E:** Explain to the patron why they are being asked to leave.
- **A:** Appeal to the person to do as requested.
- **C:** Confirm that they are refusing to leave.
- **T:** Take appropriate action.

Dealing with Violent Incidents

Due to the nature of the role played by security operatives in maintaining a safe environment for patrons of the venue you will sometimes face the risk of dealing with incidents of violence. While every effort is made to reduce this risk and mitigate the effects of violence security officers must be aware that the risk exists in their place of work.

A few points to note:

- In incidents of violence we support our security team in their actions taken to protect yourself, your colleagues, other patrons or the venue itself.

- You must remember their duty of care to yourself, your colleagues and the patrons of the venue. You have a duty to consider how your actions effect your own safety as well as the safety of others. This can also mean a failure to act.

- We do not expect security staff members to put themselves in inappropriate levels of danger. While there is a duty of care to our patrons our primary concern is your safety and that of your colleagues. When dealing with large scale incidents of violence we do not expect you to intervene until sufficient support has arrived to enable you to manage the incident at a reasonable level of safety.

- When managing incidents of violence reasonable force only can be used in all circumstances. Our interpretation of reasonable force is discussed later in this manual. At all times you retain your legal right to protect yourself and others from assault and we authorise all members of our security team to act on behalf of the venue.

- When in the course of your duty you are required to physically eject a patron you must be aware that you are wholly responsible for that person's safety throughout the process.

- To ensure both staff and patron safety and to maintain consistency when dealing with incidents we employ a range of primary and secondary control measures to prevent and detect violent incidents. We expect that you utilise these controls where possible when managing violent incidents. We also expect that all security staff continually and dynamically assess situations in which they are involved.

Primary and secondary controls

These are control measures that we have put in place as an organisation to assist the security team in keeping the level of risk associated with violence at an acceptable level. We expect that the security team utilises these control measures where applicable. This control measures include:

Control	Commentary
Risk assessment	We have designed a comprehensive risk assessment for the venue covering all aspects of work. This highlights all appropriate risk controls across the business. A summarised version of this risk assessment specifically relating to the security function can be found at the back of this manual. The full risk assessment can be accessed in the security control room.
CCTV	As detailed above we have CCTV and mobile CCTV units throughout the venue. These can be used a deterrence. Security

	staff should know their location and be aware of them when dealing with patrons.
Two-way radios	Every security team member is issued with a two-way radio. The radios act both as a visual deterrence to aggressive behaviour and as communication tool in the management of incidents.
Security equipment and PPE	The security equipment and PPE form part of our responsive measures when dealing with incidents. All security staff are provided with the right level of equipment to conduct their role.
Staffing levels	The staffing level for each night is determined in advance by the Head of Security. It is based on a guideline figure from the Code of Practice for Indoor events 1998. We always ensure our actual staffing level exceed the guidelines by a minimum of 30%.
Training	We provide initial induction and safety training to all staff before they begin work. This training is mandatory. We then provide operational training as soon as is practicable. Refresher training is regularly scheduled to ensure the skill levels of security staff do not deteriorate.

Dynamic Risk Assessment

Dynamic risk assessment is the process by which we continually assess ongoing situations. We do this so that we are constantly managing the situation at an appropriate level. The dynamic risk assessment model also gives us a framework around which we can describe our actions afterwards in our reporting procedures. The dynamic risk assessment model we use at ABC venue is SAOR©:

- **Scan:** do not run or rush into situations. Take the time to scan the entire situation.
- **Assess:** assess the type and level of risk involved in terms to the task at hand, the individuals involved and the environment in which the incident is happening.
- **Options:** evaluate your own options. What primary and secondary controls do you have at your disposal.
- **Response:** Based on the risks assessed and the options available to you what is the most appropriate response. Bear in mind that to stand back and observe may be a response in some circumstances.

All incidents of conflict must be fully reported to the Control Room to be recorded in the Security Event Log. Any incident which requires a patron to be asked to leave or where force has been used or witnessed must also be recorded using an incident report form.

Reasonable Force

All security team members will receive specific training in the area of reasonable force and its application to their role. There are a number of reasons why security operatives may be required and legally allowed to use reasonable force in the course of their role including:

- To protect themselves from injury or assault
- To protect any other person from injury or assault
- To protect the venue from theft, damage or trespass
- To make a lawful arrest where an arrestable offence has been committed in their presence.

Reasonable force has been generally defined in Irish law as; "the minimum amount of force required to maintain your safety in each circumstance". In order for force to be considered reasonable it must have 4 key ingredients. It must be:

- **Proportionate:** a proportionate response to the level of force that is perceived to be faced by the individual.
- **Legal:** carried out for one of the reasons outlined in the section above
- **Acceptable:** acceptable based on the individuals experience training and perceived level of risk.
- **Necessary:** other alternatives would not have worked and there was no option to retreat.

Force continuum

While we endeavour at all times to manage situations in a non-physical way there will always be occasions where a higher level of force may be required. It is for this reason that we expect all of our security team members are aware of the various levels of force available to them and in what circumstances they may be used. ABC Nightclub will not tell the security team which level of force to use as it will be specific to each individual based on the reasonable force model above. We will however show the force continuum.

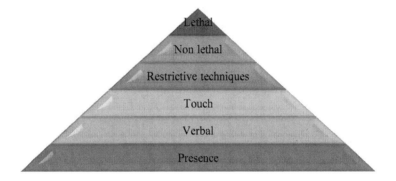

Presence: Security operatives may use body language, gestures or positioning to reduce risk in situations and deter potential conflict

Verbal skills: The use of verbal de-escalation techniques, customer service skills and communications equipment to manage incidents at low levels.

Touch: The use of light physical touch to gain attention, guide patrons or maintain person space.

Restrictive techniques: The use of restrictive and non-restrictive controls to manage physical behaviour. This level includes up to the use of pain compliance and restrictive controls to manage a patron's behaviour in high risk situations.

Impact: An emergency response may require the use of impact techniques to temporarily distract a violent patron so that a lower level of force may be employed. This level includes the use of any impact strikes or the use of impact tools. This level falls outside the scope of the professional service delivered by the security team at ABC nightclub and should only be considered in an absolute emergency.

Lethal force: This level falls outside the scope of this training manual and the expected response of the ABC security team. If the security team members have specific questions about this level of force, we advise that they seek independent legal advice on the subject

All security operatives will undergo a reasonable force briefing session at the beginning of their employment with the Head of Security. This session will be scenario based and include an assessment. Any member of the security team who has any questions around the use of force or reasonable force should direct them to the Head of Security.

Physical intervention

All security team members will be provided with training on physical intervention and transport skills which enable them to safely and professionally manage violent patrons. Security staff are given a set of principles and skills which assist them in selecting the correct and safe option when dealing with violent patrons.

While the training will teach specific knowledge and skills beyond the remit of this manual there is a need to give some general guidelines here also:

- Where the security team are required to use physical techniques to manage situations they must be aware that both the venue and the individual security team member have a duty of care to the patron throughout the incident.
- The use of pain compliant techniques is only to be used where there are no reasonable alternatives.
- The use of physical intervention techniques where the patron is held on the ground carry a very high level of risk are only to be used in an emergency. Where a situation does result in the patron ending up on the ground we will endeavour to move the patron to an alternative position as soon as it is safe to do so for the security team. Where a patron ends up in the prone position they will be transferred to an alternative position immediately.
- The use of single person techniques is not condoned and are only to be used in an emergency.
- The use of any head control or restraint above the shoulder is absolutely not condoned. From the training provided a range of alternative options will be taught. Any use of a head control (choke, strangle etc) will be fully investigated through the disciplinary process.

- The use of strikes is not condoned and are only to be used in an emergency when there are no alternatives to preserve the safety of the security operative.

- There must be ongoing communication and de-escalation between the security team member and the patron throughout the use of force situation.

- Security staff are expected to challenge and report any perceived use of excessive force by other security team members. Reports can be made confidentially to the Head of Security.

Calling the Gardaí

Where it is deemed necessary to refer a patron to the Gardaí due to their behaviour this decision will be made by the Head of Security. No other member of security should contact the Gardaí in relation to incidents which occur within the venue unless in a personal capacity. The Head of Security will be the point of contact for the venue in all dealings with Gardaí. Where it is required for a security team member to attend a Garda station to give a statement in relation to an incident they will be accompanied to the station by the Head of Security and will be paid for any time spent giving the statement.

Recording of Incidents

Writers Note:

The documentation of incidents at the time or as soon afterwards is critical for your venue. Initial customer issues may be called into the venue the following morning and it is essential that the management team has the information to deal with the issue readily available.

It is also important that incidents are being documented in a professional and consistent manner. These incidents may be required for legal proceedings far into the future and long after the staff member has left employment.

We require all incidents which require security intervention to be recorded in the Security Event Log as soon as they occur. An example of the Security Event Log can be found in the appendices. Incidents can be relayed to the control room operator by the security operative as they happen or as soon as is practical afterwards. The radio call must include;

- Your radio call sign
- The nature of the event i.e. refusal, removal from the venue etc,
- A description of the individual involved
- The actions of the security operative

The type of events which must be recorded include:

- Refusal of entry

- Aggressive behaviour at entry

- Prohibited items found during a search (excluding alcohol)

- Complaints

- Accidents and first aid

- Requests for assistance

- Management requests

- Requests to leave

- Removals

- Any use of force situation

At the end of each shift a team debrief will take place where the Head of Security will review each incident with the security staff involved and decide if a full incident report is required.

Security Notebooks

Every security team member is issued with a personal notebook. Details of an incident and witness details can be recorded in the security notebook at the time of the event for transfer to an incident report later. Details such as contact information for lost property and initial details of customer issues should be recorded at the time in the notebook. Notebooks are individual to the security staff member and should not be shared. Notebooks should be stored securely at the venue and not brought home after work. Lost, stolen or damaged notebooks should be reported immediately to the control room via radio and an incident report completed. As notebooks can contain the personal information of many of our customers they must be kept on your person while on duty and stored security in the security control room when not in use,

Incident reporting

In order to maintain an effective communication route from the security team to venue management it is important that the security operative records and reports incidents in an accurate and concise manner. An adequate supply of incident report forms is located in the security control room. Incident reports form a key part of our risk reduction and risk management strategy. All of your reports are reviewed by the Head of Security and other members of management and used to assist us in monitoring the effectiveness of our policies, procedures and training. They are also used where we may have to provide evidence in criminal and civil legal proceedings. For these reasons we need to ensure that they are professionally written, consistent and factual,

Guidelines for security report writing

The following guidelines should be followed for all incident reports:

- Reports will be written as soon as possible after the incident. All reports must be completed prior to finishing your shift. Exceptions to this will be made where a security operative has been injured or is medically unfit to complete the report.
- All reports must be completed using the incident report template. An example of the incident report can be found in the appendices

- Reports should be written in black ink for copying and scanning purposes
- Use plain English and limit technical phrases. Do not use slang, abbreviations or any language that could be interpreted as being offensive or discriminatory.
- Avoid stating opinions without evidence. Reports must be a factual account of what you saw and did. Where you have been 'told' something by another person this should be recorded as such.
- Use the 24hour clock when referring to time and full version format of any day and date information.
- Write clearly and legibly throughout the report. Where you are concerned about your standard of handwriting, spelling etc we can facilitate the use of a computer to type your report. We may also have your report scribed by a senior member of staff and recorded as such.
- Do not erase and part of the report using correction fluid or colour over errors. If you make an error place a bracket around the error, cross a line through the affected section and initial the error.
- Always sign and date your report

Incident Reports

Incident reports are factual witness accounts of an incident. They should be correctly structured and in a standardised format. Reports should be divided into 3 sections:

Section 1: Introduction of incident.
Section 2: Main body of report.
Section 3: Conclusion of incident
The below format is the standard layout that we expect to see delivered in all incident reports.

Incident Report Format

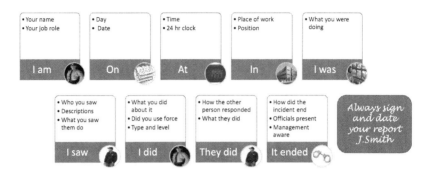

An example of a completed incident report is available for guidance in the appendices section. This example is also posted on the security control room wall for ongoing reference.

Descriptions

A full and detailed description of each member of the public involved in an incident must be provided. The standard model we use for physical descriptions is SABHHIC. The details for this model are outlined below. Where a person's skin colour or ethnicity is of benefit from a descriptive point of view the international classification, system can be used.

		SABHHIC
S	Sex	Male or female
A	Age	Use 5-year blocks (e.g. 20 to 25) and approximate
B	Build	Thin, medium, heavy
H	Height	Use imperial or metric measure and approximate
H	Hair	Length, colour and style
I	Identifying marks	Scars, tattoos, accents, other identifiers
C	Clothes	Colour, style, type and brand. Top to bottom

Identity Classifications	
IC1	White
IC2	Mediterranean
IC3	Black
IC4	Asian
IC5	Arabic
IC6	Indian

Section 4: Safety and Emergency Procedures

In the event of any safety issue, accident or emergency taking place at the venue it is essential the security team on duty respond in a co-ordinated, efficient and professional manner. The types of emergencies detailed in this section are foreseeable based on the risk assessment carried out for the venue, however the list is not exhaustive. Any member of security can raise a health and safety issue at any point for inclusion on the risk register or emergency plans. All issues will be discussed at senior management levels.

General accident prevention

We expect that all members of security work to recognise and prevent potential accidents. We take a proactive approach to safety in the venue and expect you to do the same. If you identify a hazard, we expect that you take reasonable steps to make it safe and communicate this issue to the control room. We provide cleaning staff on duty at all times that the venue is open, and they can be contacted via radio to deal with any spillages or other minor cleaning issues.

Spillages and broken glass

Spillages of drinks and broken glass as a result of dropped drinks have the potential to cause slips and falls as well as cuts. We employ a team of glass collection staff to patrol the floor areas and collect empty glasses. However, on busy nights some areas may be missed or have a faster than normal build-up of glasses. If you observe empty glasses built up, please notify a glass collector on patrol. Glass collectors are not equipped with radios and so will need to be personally notified. If you observe patrons acting recklessly or dangerously near a build-up of glasses, we expect that you speak to the patrons and make the glasses safe until you can identify a glass collector.

Where a security team member identifies a spillage, the following process should be followed:

- Stand over the affected area and highlight the hazard to patrons using your torch. Guide patrons around the hazard.
- Notify a cleaner that you require a yellow wet floor/hazard sign brought to your location.
- Stay with the cleaner while they remove the hazard and ensure no patrons enter the area while cleaning is ongoing.

Trip hazards

Patrons can sometimes create trip hazards by leaving belongings in areas where they may be fallen over. Security staff should be observant for any items left on the floor throughout the venue. Critical areas for attention are fire escape routes and congestion areas such as stairways and the dancefloor. Where items are identified on the floor you should attempt to identify the owner of the property in the vicinity. If the owner cannot be found, then the property should be treated as found property. It is not permitted for patrons to leave bags, coats, shoes or any other property on the ground where they are standing or on the dancefloor while dancing. These patrons should be directed to the cloakroom with their property.

Footwear

Footwear must be worn by patrons at all times on the property. Where security staff identify patrons, who are not wearing shoes they should be directed to put on shoes immediately. Security should stay with the patron until the shoes are put on. Where a patron refuses the will be asked to leave. If a patron has a foot injury or other issue which makes it difficult to wear shoes they can be escorted by security to the first aid room where a limited supply of flat shoes is available. While escorting a patron with no shoes on they should use their torch to highlight the ground and ensure it is free of glass and other hazards that may further injure the patrons' feet.

First Aid

While we always attempt to reduce the risk of injury to our patrons it can never be eliminated. We provide a comprehensive first aid provision at ABC Nightclub to ensure that we provide the highest level of care to our patrons. This includes the provision of several first aid trained staff on duty at all times and a dedicated first aid and welfare area.

First aid staff

All of the first aid staff will be trained to First Aid Responder level and will receive periodic refresher training to ensure their certification skills remain up to date and in line with changes in practice in this area. First aid staff shall be positioned strategically by the Head of Security to ensure they are as mobile as possible to respond to accidents. For large events there will be dedicated first aid staff positioned in the first aid room throughout the event. We also have a small number of staff who are trained to Emergency First Responder level which is a higher level of training. There will a minimum of one EFR level staff member on duty at all times. These staff will respond as normal to minor first aid incidents and provide a supervisory and management role for more serious accident.

Once a security staff member has served 6 months or more as an employee they are entitled to apply to join the first aid team. Should you be selected for this role ABC Nightclub will provide training through a third-party supplier to you free of charge. Selection of the first aid team is based on business need and is at the discretion of the Head of Security.

First aid equipment

All security staff must carry disposable gloves on their person at all times. In addition to this first aid equipment (50-person boxes) are located throughout the venue for ease of access by first aid staff.

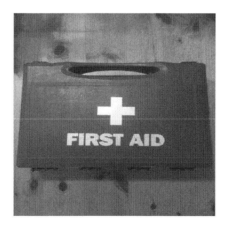

All of our first aid boxes are the same style as the photograph below and are signified by a first aid sign (also shown below)

Location of first aid equipment

Ref	Area	Exact location
1	Front door	Wall mounted in a cabinet to the right of the door just inside main entrance.
2	Rear entrance	Wall mounted in a cabinet to the left of the door just inside rear entrance.
3	Security control room	Wall mounted inside the door of the control room
4	Bar 1	Mounted on a wall bracket under Bar 1 next to the dishwasher
5	Bar 2	Mounted on a wall bracket on the rear wall next to the spirit shelf
6	Managers office	Wall mounted on the right-hand side of the office just inside the main door

All first aid kits are checked at the beginning of each shift by the assigned first aiders before the venue opens and are re-stocked from the supply in the first aid room. First aid replenishment orders are completed monthly if required and sourced through our third-party supplier.

First aid room

ABC's nightclub provides a fully equipped first aid area adjacent our security control room. We use this area to assess and treat accident victims in a safe and secure environment. We also use it to supervise patrons who are overly intoxicated and require a medical assessment to ensure they are safe to leave the premises. The first aid room is equipped in line with current Health and Safety Authority guidelines and includes:

- 2 x mobile 50-person first aid kits
- 1x mobile burns kit
- 1x Defibrillator
- 1x Wheelchair
- Access to sterile water
- Dedicated landline with speaker phone
- 2x first aid beds
- Blankets
- Towels
- Vomit bags

Our first aid room is kept locked for security reasons however it can be accessed by any member of security. There is constant CCTV monitoring in the first aid room for security reasons however this recording is housed on a separate DVR with limited access for privacy reasons.

Response to accidents

This following procedure is to be following on finding an accident or potential medical incident:

- The security team member must immediately apply their own gloves before attending to the accident.

- If the casualty has a minor injury such as small cut etc, escort the casualty to the first aid room.

- Contact the control room on the radio and advise them that you are leaving your position with a medical incident. The control room operator will monitor you on CCTV and arrange a first aid person to meet you at the medical room

- If a casualty is found on the ground contact the control room on your radio and request a first aider to your location. The control room will monitor you on CCTV and dispatch the closest first aid person.

- If the casualty is on the ground do not lift, move or assist the patron to get up.

- Once the first aid person has arrived deliver a quick briefing to them and await their instruction.

- If the first aider requires further assistance you should request this on the radio to control and allow them to deliver medical treatment.

- If they do not require assistance you should begin to manage the crowd at the scene and create a sterile area free of patrons for the treatment.

Accident and Incident Scene Preservation

In the event of a serious incident or accident at the venue it will probably be required to preserve the scene until the arrival of the relevant authorities. All major accidents/incident responses will be co-ordinated by the Head of Security.

- Immediately after an accident /incident the security team will seal off the area using tape or some type of barrier.
- The Head of Security will position members of the security team in static positions around the scene.
- The relevant authorities will be contacted by the Head of Security. No member of the security team is authorised to contact the authorities unless specifically asked to do so by venue management.
- Management will decide in conjunction with the Head of Security whether to close and clear the venue pending the arrival of authorities or await their arrival first.
- Nobody should be allowed into the sealed area without a valid reason until the arrival of the relevant authorities. Exceptions to this would include persons administering first aid etc.
- Nothing should be inserted into or removed from the scene however irrelevant it may seem.
- Photographs of the scene will be taken by security operatives nominated by the Head of Security.
- Every member of staff involved in the accident/incident must produce an incident report.
- Do not speak to anybody apart from the relevant authorities about the incident.
- Every assistance will be given to the relevant authorities on arrival.

- When the authorities arrive the name of the person taking control of the incident must be recorded.
- Once the authorities have left an accident investigation will take place

Accident investigation

Once the authorities have left the venues own accident investigation will take place. The venue has an accident investigation kit which is located on the top shelf in the security control room. It contains:

- PPE: Disposable gloves and boot covers.
- 2x cameras: One is a digital camera so that the photos can be uploaded to a computer and attached to an electronic report. The second camera is a disposable single use camera to produce hard copy photos in case anything happens to the digital copies, the SD card gets corrupted or the batteries die in the digital camera.
- Measuring tape: For scale on accident scenes and also to show the size of a damaged area.
- Graph paper: To sketch out an accident/incident scene and mark in key objects or positions of people. This is to scale the drawing to the scene using the measuring tape (1 square = 0.5m for example) to make a sketch more accurate.
- Barrier tape: 50ft of barrier tape to cordon off a scene while it's awaiting clean up or while the investigation is ongoing

- Bio hazard kit: For cleaning up the after an accident. It is likely there will be body fluid such as blood or vomit at the scene requiring a more hygienic method of cleaning than normal.
- Sharpie: To number marker signs or make markings on surfaces.
- Flash cards: To create marker signs and write smaller notes for attachment to a later report. Can also be used to take witness details
- Zip-lock bags: To collect and seal items such as damaged equipment that might need to be kept safely for later use or inspection.

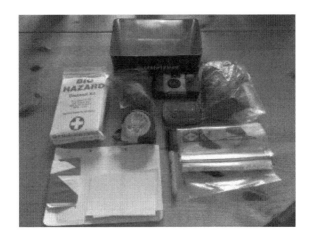

Once the accident investigation has been completed the Head of Security will issue an instruction to open the area again. In minor instances this may take a few minutes however for major accidents or incidents it may be a number of hours. This may necessitate security staff working additional hours after the normal finish time.

Escalation Procedure

In the event of a serious accident or incident the security escalation procedure should be followed.

Any serious accident/incident involving patrons or staff of the venue will be immediately notified via phone call or text message to the venue management if not on duty.

The Head of Security is the only person who has the authority to represent the company position to the authorities and will speak to venue management on behalf of the security team.

As soon as is reasonably and safely practicable following an incident the security operative will write a comprehensive report of the incident. A copy of this should be given to the Head of Security and venue management as soon as possible.

Industrial Injury Procedure

In the event of an accident or incident occurring at work which results in an injury to an employee the industrial injury procedure should be followed. The venue may at its own discretion decide to pay any medical or other costs incurred by the employee. Payments made at the venues discretion in relation to industrial injuries in no way admit liability on behalf of the venue.

The Head of Security shall accompany the injured operative for further medical attention if required.

As soon as is reasonably practicable after the incident a written report should be made detailing the full circumstances in the situation.

In all instances where a security officer is injured the Head of Security will undertake a full investigation into the incident. This is to prevent further recurrences and put in place preventative controls.

Fire Safety

A major part of the security team's role is to ensure the fire safety of the venue. Due to the large number of people with access to the venue and the level of flammable material within the club there will always be a risk of fire.

The security team will take a proactive approach to fire safety in its patrolling and observation of patrons. The security team will take a zero-tolerance approach to fire safety issues and remove any patrons who are behaving in a dangerous manner.

Fire precautions

The security team will take the following precautions regarding fire safety:

- Ensure all fire exits remain clear and unobstructed

- Ensure all fire equipment is clear, unobstructed and not tampered with or used maliciously
- Deal with all potential fire hazards in a proactive manner
- Be aware of all fire points and fire equipment within the venue.
- Understand their responsibility in an evacuation.

Fire Equipment

ABC Nightclub is fully equipped with a complete set of firefighting equipment throughout the venue. Fire extinguishers are located at fire points throughout the nightclub which are clearly signed with fire point signage and a fire extinguisher sign. The majority of fire points also have a break glass unit adjacent to them with a fire action notice next to it.

Security operatives should be familiar with the location, type and suitability of each type of fire extinguisher. A full tour of the fire equipment will be undertaken with each security team member before starting work at ABC Nightclub.

Fire safety training

Fire safety and evacuation training will be given to all employees at induction and involve the immediate action to be taken on alarm and the evacuation procedure. Periodically ABC nightclub will provide training through a third-party provider in advanced fire safety including the use of fire extinguishers. The training is on a voluntary basis and is not mandatory to attend. This training will be made available to you at no cost should you wish to undertake it. Undertaking this training supplies you with additional skills which you may use in the event of an emergency. Completion of the training does not place any expectation on you from the company that you attempt to fight a fire. Your safety is paramount always and our immediate actions and evacuation plan reflect this principle.

Fire alarm activation

In the event of a fire alarm activation within the venue the following procedure will be followed:

- The Head of Security will proceed directly to the security control room repeater panel and check the location of the alarm
- The control room operator will have already relayed the location of the alarm to the nearest available security operative.
- The nearest available security operative will investigate the alarm location.
- While the alarm is in activation the remainder of the security team will remain on standby in case an evacuation may be required.
- A 'CODE ORANGE' radio call will be made by the Head of Security to put all staff on standby for evacuation.
- If a false alarm is to be declared it will be done by the dual authentication of the nearest available security operative and the Head of Security via the CCTV system.

- If the fire is confirmed as real, then the evacuation procedure will apply.

Fire

If a member of the security team discovers a fire on the premises an immediate and efficient response is required. We use the R.A.C.E. system for dealing with a fire.

R.A.C.E.

- **R: Rescue** – Rescue those in immediate danger from the fire.
- **A: Alert** – Use the nearest fire call point to activate the alarm and follow this up with a radio call to the control room. The fire services will be contacted by the Head of Security.
- **C: Confine** - Close all doors and windows in the area and along the evacuation route as you clear patrons from the venue.
- **E: Extinguish-** If you are trained and the appropriate extinguisher is available you may consider extinguishing the fore. This will only be attempted when the fire is stable ad contained and a safe evacuation route is present.

Evacuation

If an evacuation is required, it needs to be done in a controlled manner to ensure staff and patron safety.

- On receipt of a fire alarm or radio call of a fire at the venue the above evacuation procedure will begin

- A **Code Orange** radio call will be broadcast by the Head of Security. On hearing this all staff should stand by their closest exit and prepare to evacuate.

- Venue management will ensure all bars and cloakrooms are immediately closed however the music or entertainment will continue.

- When the fire is confirmed as a real a **Code Black** radio message will be broadcast. This is signal to begin the evacuation.

- The music or entertainment will be stopped, and an emergency message will be broadcast to patrons by venue management.

- The security team should open all fire exit doors and begin to evacuate patrons to the assembly point.

- A security team member will be designated to ensure the toilets are clear.

- When your area of responsibility is clear move to the assembly point and report to the Head of Security.

- If patrons attempt to re-enter the venue you will prevent them from doing so and long as it is safe for you to do so.

- If a patron becomes aggressive or violent towards you or runs inside the venue do not become involved or follow them in.

- Do not leave the assembly area until instructed to do so by the Head of Security

Assembly Point

- The primary assembly point is located at:

_____

- The secondary assembly point for ABC nightclub is located at:

_____

Section 5: Administrative procedures

Writers Note:

This section of the manual is the administrative procedures section. It has less security related policies and procedures and more procedures aimed at ensuring the team can operate at its optimum. In this section it is important to set your procedures for items such as staff background checks, new starter procedures and staff training. It is also important to discuss important company polices such as equality and bullying.

The section will also contain more mundane procedures such as how employees can call in sick where they can take a cigarette break. It is not a replacement for a staff handbook or an employment contract, but it is designed as a quick reference guide for new and existing staff.

New employees

All new employees including security staff will receive role specific induction training from their line manager. This manual will form the basis of that induction training for members of the security team. At the point of receiving this manual all new employees in the security team will have already received:

- A contract of employment including terms and conditions
- A new starter pack containing relevant documents
- A uniform and equipment supply.

Probationary period

All security employees are hired subject to a 6-month probationary period. In that time either party can choose to end the employment with a weeks' notice for any reason. This clause is contained in the employment contract of all security employees. Examples of issues which may lead to termination during the probationary period include:

- Consistent lateness
- Unprofessional behaviour
- Excessive use of force
- Gross misconduct

Background screening

All security employees will already be in possession of a Private Security Authority Door Supervisor licence prior to employment. Criminal background checks will already have been completed as part of this licencing process.

However, in addition to a criminal background check ABC will also conduct a 5-year employment screening of all security operatives. This will involve contacting all previous employers in the past 5 years to verify the employment period and the reason for leaving. All security operatives are employed subject to satisfactory completion of this screening process.

Licence renewals

The renewal of individual security licences is the responsibility of the security operative. Once hired all security operatives must lodge a copy of their licence in their staff file. The expiry date will be stored by the Head of Security in a calendar. Reminders will be given to security staff via email at 3 months, 2 months and 1 month before the licence expires. Should a security operative allow their licence to expire without renewing it then they will be suspended without pay pending receipt of the new licence.

ABC Nightclub operates a scheme whereby the company can arrange to fund the security operative licence renewal cost upfront and the cost can be deducted at €10 per week out from salary over a period of time. The security operative must request this facility in advance of the renewal.

Commitment to training

Writers Note:

A training policy for security staff is essential. It should set out the view of the venue on initial and ongoing training. It will also state the type, duration and interval of the training and who will conduct the training.

ABC Nightclub believes in providing a quality security service to its staff and guests. We do this primarily by providing security operatives who are trained to a level which exceeds all industry standards. We believe that in the training and development of our staff lies the future of our venue. We are committed to using the best qualified trainers in the industry to deliver the best training courses to our security team thereby allowing us to deliver the best quality service to our guests.

Training Policy

ABC Nightclub provide training to all of its security operatives relevant to the roles they will undertake. We provide induction training to all new employees as soon as is practicable following their employment. This will be done prior to the employee's first operational shift. We provide refresher training at regular intervals to all security operatives to ensure that all training is current changes to best practice are communicated regularly

ABC Nightclub have nominated a training officer who will oversee the training regime within the security team. The Head of Security also acts as the training officer. The training officer organises and co-ordinates all training and where possible conducts the training sessions themselves. Any specialist training which requires a qualified trainer will be carried out by our external training partners. They also ensure that all training is recorded accurately in an employee's file.

Records of all training will be kept. The records will be signed by both the employee and the trainer and will be retained by the company in each employees file. It will be the duty of the training officer to ensure that these records are kept current.

Training curriculum

Security operatives will undertake the below training curriculum:

Training	Length of service	Intervals
Induction	First shift	N/A
Manual/person handling	First week	Annually
Crowd management	First week	2 years
Conflict resolution	First 2 weeks (restricted duty until then)	2 years
Physical intervention	First month (restricted duty until then)	Annually
Fire warden	Optional after 6 months	2 years
First aid	Optional after 6 months	2 years

All training is paid for by ABC nightclub and security operatives are paid for their time attending this training.

Absence

A full absence policy is available in the staff handbook however, for ease of reference for the security team the procedure is outlined below. Employees absent from work without prior permission must notify the company within 2 hours of their scheduled starting time. All absences other than certified illnesses, compassionate, annual or written leave of absence approved by management, will be subject to disciplinary action in accordance disciplinary procedure.

Security operatives who will be absent for work for any reason must contact the Head of Security via phone as soon as they become aware of the absence. The Head of Security's phone number is located in the emergency contacts appendix at the back of this manual. A text message is not sufficient for notifying absence. If the Head of Security is not available, the Duty Manager will be contacted.

Lateness

If a security operative is running late for work, they must contact the Head of Security as soon as they become aware of the issue so that alternative arrangement can be made at the venue. The security operative must call the Head of Security's phone. A text message is not sufficient to notify lateness. The security operative should let the Head of Security know of the approximate time of arrival.

No Show

If you do not show for a shift ABC Nightclub will assume that there has been an emergency which has prevented, you from attending. We will attempt to contact to you 3 times by phone within 30 minutes of being late for your scheduled shift time. If you fail to answer we will assume that there may be an emergency and will attempt to contact your emergency contacts from the staff file.

It is very important that security operatives notify us of any inability to attend work to avoid the above process being implemented.

Smoking

Security operatives will get a short refreshment break at some time during the shift. If a security operative chooses to have a cigarette or e-cigarette during this time we request that they do the following.

- Use the designated staff smoking area at the rear of the building
- Do not use the public smoking area.
- Do not invite members of the public to the staff smoking area.
- Dispose of any cigarette litter in the ash tray provided
- Return any glasses or cups used to the bar area and do not leave them in the smoking area.

Alcohol

As per our employment contracts the consumption of alcohol or any other intoxicant before or during work is strictly prohibited. Any evidence that a security operative has consumed alcohol or other intoxicants before or after work will result in the person being sent home immediately and being invited to a follow up investigation.

Off duty entry

Security operatives are free to attend ABC Nightclub on their nights off. All staff are given free entry for themselves plus one guest once a week. We remind all staff that their behaviour on the premises while off duty is expected to reflect the fact that they are an employee. Any behaviour from the off-duty security operative which the Head of Security deems to be unsuitable will result in the person and their guest being asked to leave. This may result in disciplinary action upon return to work or revocation of staff entry privileges.

Equality

ABC Nightclub is an equal opportunities business. As such it is committed to equality of opportunity for existing and potential employees and customers. ABC Nightclub promotes an environment which provides for equal opportunities for all staff and customers where their dignity is protected and respected at all times.

All persons regardless of gender, marital status, family status, race, religious beliefs, sexual orientation, disability, age or membership of the travelling community will be provided with equality of access to employment, access and service.

All security operatives have an important role to play in ensuring equality of opportunity throughout the organisation. It is also recognised that individual employees on behalf of ABC Nightclub have responsibilities in law and:

• are required to co-operate with any measures introduced by the company to promote equal opportunities.

• must not themselves, either directly or indirectly, discriminate, harass or intimidate fellow employees or customers in any way.

Bullying

The Employer is committed to providing a safe and secure working environment that is free of bullying and harassment (including sexual harassment) and within which all members of staff will be treated with dignity and respect. All employees have an obligation to prevent and eliminate bullying and harassment. This policy is applicable to all employees (permanent and temporary) both in the workplace and at associated events such as meetings, training courses and other company functions whether on or off site.

It also applies to contractors, customers and other business contacts which employees might reasonably come into contact within the course of their employment.

The company acknowledges the right of all employees to be treated with fairness, dignity and respect and to a work environment free from bullying and harassment. Every employee has an obligation to be aware of the effects their behaviour has on others. It is imperative that all employees respect the dignity of every colleague and be conscious of behaviour which may cause offence.

Any instances of bullying/harassment will be dealt with in an effective and efficient manner. Cases where the behaviour is proved to be repeated and consistent causing unnecessary stress and anxiety will be considered as gross misconduct and will be subject to disciplinary action up to and including dismissal.

Definition of Bullying/Harassment

Bullying/Harassment are defined as any form of repeated, unwelcome and unacceptable conduct that can be regarded as offensive, humiliating or intimidation. An individual can be harassed on grounds of race, religious belief, national ethnic origin, gender, sexual orientation, age civil status, disability or membership of the travelling community.

The Harassment can include conduct offensive to a reasonable person e.g. Oral or written slurs, physical contact, gestures, jokes, displaying pictures, flags/emblems, graffiti or other material which state or imply prejudicial attitudes which are offensive to fellow employees.

Other examples of bullying behaviour include:

- Personal insults and name calling

- Persistent unjustified criticism and sarcasm

- Public or private humiliation

- Shouting at employees in public and/or private sneering

- Instantaneous rage often over trivial issues

- Unfair delegation of duties and responsibilities

- Setting impossible deadlines

- Unnecessary work interference

- Making it difficult for employees to have access to necessary work information.

- Aggression

- Not giving credit for work contribution

- Continuously refusing reasonable requests without good reason

- Intimidation and threats in general

Sexual harassment can be defined as conduct towards another person that is sexual in nature or has a sexual dimension and is unwelcome to the recipient.

Examples of this type of harassment include:

•   Sexual gestures

•   Displaying sexual suggestive objectives, pictures, calendars or sending suggestive or pornographic correspondence (including e-mail)

•   Unwelcome sexual comments or jokes

•   Unwelcome physical contacts such as pinching, unnecessary touching etc.

The above examples are not exhaustive and only serve as guideline to employees. Each case will be taken in isolation and dealt with in the appropriate manner.

Claims of bullying and harassment will be dealt with under the grievance and disciplinary procedure.

Grievance and disciplinary issues

Writers Note:

Once again it is important to stress that this isn't a staff employment handbook or a HR handbook. It is a manual for procedures that are important for security staff only.

However, when it comes to grievance and disciplinary issues it is important to let staff know what to expect if a complaint is made.

It does not need to be overly detailed in this section as the HR policies and procedures should be in a staff handbook or HR manual. It is an overview only of what to expect for security operatives.

The full grievance and disciplinary policy and procedures are available in the staff handbook and HR Managers office. It is however important for security operatives to note what will happen in the event of a complaint being made about their behaviour.

Complaints and grievances

ABC nightclub differentiates between grievances and complaints by the source of the issue. Grievances are raised internally by other staff members and complaints are those raised by customers. Regardless of the source of the claim each incident will be reviewed on its merits and investigated thoroughly.

In the event of a complaint or grievance about a member of the security team which the management feels may have merit then the operative in question will be made aware before any investigation begins. The Head of Security will first review the security operative's incident report of the incident and any other reports. If no reports exist, then the Head of Security will arrange for the security operative to provide one in the first instance. Once the security operatives report has been received then any other evidence such as CCTV will be reviewed. If upon review of the evidence the Head of Security feels it may warrant a formal investigation it will be handed over to HR for further action.

If the Head of Security feels there is no case to answer they will inform both the security operative and the HR Manager of this and provide a written report to this effect. Security operatives should be made aware that ABC Nightclub will review every incident that is reported. The review of an incident does not imply any wrongdoing or guilt on behalf of a security operative.

In certain circumstances where a grievance creates the risk of further issues in the workplace ABC nightclub may suspend one or both parties involved in the interest of completing the investigation. Suspension does not imply and wrongdoing or guilt on either party. All suspensions will be made on full pay pending the outcome of the investigation.

We ask that all security operatives make themselves aware of the full grievance and disciplinary procedure and their rights contained within it.

Scheduling

The security team schedule is posted weekly on a Friday in the security office. It is posted 4 weeks in advance. From time to time due

149

to late bookings or events we may need to change this at short notice. We will contact the individual security operative immediately by phone in this case and confirm his/her availability. Shift changes at more than 1-week notice are mandatory unless previously booked off. Shift changes at less than 1 week are discretionary however we would appreciate that security operatives can assist where possible. Once the schedule is completed and posted on a Friday an electronic copy is also emailed to each security team member by the Head of Security. Any shift changes once confirmed on the phone are also emailed to the relevant security operative.

Time off requests

ABC Nightclub will endeavour to facilitate time off requests where possible. However, the requirements of the venue will supersede any time off request if multiple security operatives request the same date off. A time off request diary is held in the security control room. Security operatives are asked to write their requested dates in the diary immediately once they become aware of it. The security operative should notify the Head of Security or control room operator of the request when writing it in and this person will countersign and date the request. Time off requests will be granted on a first come first served basis unless there is an occasion of utmost importance. In such cases it should be made known to the Head of Security who will review the schedule for this date and attempt to facilitate the request. Requesting time off does not guarantee that the request will be granted.

When requesting time off please also state whether this is paid annual leave, unpaid leave or a swap of shifts that is being requested.

Shift swaps

The swapping of shifts between security operatives is only allowed once authorised by the Head of Security. Once both security operatives have agreed, and the Head of Security has authorised the change the schedule will be updated, and a new copy sent to both.

Annual Leave

Annual leave of more than two days taken together must be requested 4 weeks in advance through the time off request book and clearly marked as annual leave. No more than 2 weeks annual leave can be taken together for operational reasons

Restricted times

While leave and time off will be facilitated where possible there are specific days and week where due to operational requirements it is not possible to give time off or leave to any members of the security team. These dates will be marked clearly in the time off request diary at the start of the year and time off cannot be requested during these periods. These periods include:

- St Patricks Day
- Local festival week in May

- Halloween
- Any weekend in December
- New Year's Eve

Security team meetings

> **Writers Note**:
>
> Security team meetings are important. Yes, they cost a little money, but the benefits outweigh the cost. If you can't do it monthly, then at least do it quarterly. Have your Head of Security chair the meeting and address any issues or topics you feel security need to be made aware of. It's a chance to plan upcoming events or nights, review polices, discuss training and raise any issues. They can also be used to review previous incidents in detail. The meetings should be documented by the Head of Security to track issues in case of an incident or claim.

ABC Nightclub hold a security team meeting once a month. The meeting takes place on the first Saturday night of each month at 20.00 prior to security staff beginning work. All security staff are expected to attend this meeting each month if scheduled to work on the night. Security staff who are not scheduled to work or who have annual leave or requested time off are exempt from attending. The meeting lasts approximately one hour, and all security team members are paid for their time to attend. Security staff are asked to submit any topics or issues they wish to discuss in advance to be included in the agenda. The agenda will be sent out in the week before the meeting and all staff are encouraged to discuss any points raised. Each meeting will at a minimum cover:

- Health and safety issues
- Upcoming event planning
- Scheduling issues
- Previous incident reviews
- Training
- Policy and procedure reviews
- Any other business raised by the security team

The minutes of the meeting will be recorded and sent out in the week following the meeting. Failure to attend the security team meeting without advance notice or due cause may result in disciplinary action.

Appendix 1: Emergency contact details

EMERGENCY SERVICES: 112 or 999

Role	Contact
Head of Security	
Nightclub manager	
Reception	
Gardaí	
Fire Brigade	
Ambulance	

Appendix 2: Security sign in sheet
Security Sign In

Day:		Date:	
Controller:		Duty Mgr.:	

Name	Licence No.	Time In	Time Out	Signature

The above hours have been confirmed as accurate

Controller signature: _____ Date: _____

The above hours have been reviewed and authorised.

Head of Security: _____ Date: _____

Appendix 3: Incident Report Form
Accident & Incident Report Form

Incident Type		Date:		Time:	

Security Operative 1		Security Operative 2	
Security Operative 3		Security Operative 4	
Manager on Duty		Garda/EMT:	

Customer Details

Surname:		First Name:	
Address:			
Date of Birth:		Telephone:	

Accident/Incident Details

Accident/Incident Summary	
Injury Details	

Treatment Details (if applicable)

First Aider:		Role:	
Treatment Given			
Further Advice			

Please insert any witness details or further relevant information here

Customer signature:		Date:	
Security signature:		Date:	
Management review:		Date:	

Please provide full details of the accident or incident below including any witness statements. Attach further pages if required. Please attach any sketches, photographs or video footage of the accident or incident to this form if applicable. **(This page is for company use only and should not be viewed by or given to the customer at the time of the incident)**

I hereby declare that the statements and information contained in and attached to this form are accurate, truthful and complete, to the best of my knowledge and belief.

Security signature:		Date:	
Management review:		Date:	

Accident & Incident Report Form

Incident Type	*Trespass*	Date:	*20/09/2014*	Time:	*22.30 app.*

Security Operative 1	*John Smith*	Security Operative 2	
Security Operative 3		Security Operative 4	
Manager on Duty	*Paul Kelly*	Garda/EMT:	*N/A*

Customer Details

Surname:	*Unknown*	First Name:	
Address:			
Date of Birth:		Telephone:	

Accident/Incident Details

Accident/Incident Summary	*Male removed from the premises for trespass. Aggressive behaviour during removal.*
Injury Details	*None*

Treatment Details (if applicable)

First Aider:	*N/A*	Role:	
Treatment Given	*N/A*		
Further Advice	*N/A*		

Please insert any witness details or further relevant information here

N/A

Customer signature:	N/A	Date:	
Security signature:	John Smith	Date:	20/09/2014
Management review:	Paul Kelly	Date:	20/09/2014

Please provide full details of the accident or incident below including any witness statements. Attach further pages if required. Please attach any sketches, photographs or video footage of the accident or incident to this form if applicable. (**This page is for company use only and should not be viewed by or given to the customer at the time of the incident**)

My name is John Smith and I am a professional security operative employed by Elite Security. On Friday 20.09.2014 at approximately 22.30 I was on duty in the ABC Hotel, Main Street, Dublin 1. I was positioned in the bar and I was patrolling the stage area at this time. I was approached by the night manager Paul Kelly who informed me that a male was acting aggressively in the seated area of the bar approximately 10 metres to my left. I requested Paul Kelly to accompany me to the area.

In the bar area I observed a male (MALE 1 - IC1, approximately 20-25 years old, medium build, 5 feet 10 inches, brown hair, wearing blue jeans, a red shirt and black shoes) in the seated area shouting at other patrons. I could not see any other people with the male, so I approached MALE 1 and identified myself as a security operative from the venue. I asked MALE 1 to accompany me to the lobby where we could have a conversation about what was happening. MALE 1 refused and was becoming louder and appeared more aggressive. I asked MALE 1 why he was shouting, and he told me to "mind my own business". I informed MALE 1 that I was trying to help him but if he continued to behave in such a way he would be asked to leave. MALE 1 walked away from me and continued to shout. I again approached MALE 1 and at this point I asked him to leave the venue as his behaviour was unacceptable. MALE1 refused to leave so I informed that as per venue policy if he refused to leave he would be regarded as a trespasser and he may be removed, or the Gardaí may be called. I informed MALE 1 that if he agreed to walk with me to the door I would assist him in getting a taxi. MALE 1 again refused to leave. I consulted night Manager Paul Kelly and informed him of the situation. He informed me that he would like MALE 1 removed from the premises. I returned to MALE and informed him that he was *again being asked to leave and if he refused he would be regarded as a trespasser and would be escorted from the hotel. I confirmed with MALE 1 that he was refusing to leave. The male continued to gesture and speak aggressively towards me and I felt my safety and the safety of other patrons was at risk from this male. Using reasonable force, I applied a standard industry control technique to the male's right arm. This was necessary at that time to protect me from injury while escorting the male and was proportionate to the risk of injury I felt at that time.*

I escorted MALE 1 to the exit and led him outside. Outside of the venue I released MALE 1 once it was safe to do so. He continued to shout aggressively towards me. I informed MALE 1 that if he did not leave the area Gardaí would be called. MALE 1 left the area and walked in the direction of Side Street. I monitored the male from my position at the door until he was a safe distance I then returned to my position in the bar area.

I hereby declare that the statements and information contained in and attached to this form are accurate, truthful and complete, to the best of my knowledge and belief.

Security signature:	*John Smith*	Date:	*21/09/2014*
Management review:	*Paul Kelly*	Date:	*21/09/2014*

Appendix 5: Security Equipment Register
Security Equipment Register

Day:		Date:	

Please record the asset number of each piece of security equipment issued to each security operative. Once all equipment is returned the controller will initial the returned to control column

Name	Radio	Ear Piece	Jacket	Vest	Other	Returned to Control

Missing Equipment

Missing Item	Commentary

Controller Signature: _____ Date: _____

Appendix 6: Security Communications Log

Security Communications Log			
Date	Time	Narrative	Signature

Controller signature: _____   Date: _____

Appendix 7: Security Event Log

Date	Time	Incident Type	Physical Description	Security Operative 1	Security Operative 2

Controller signature: _____ Date: _____

Head of Security: _____ Date: _____

Appendix 8: Security Job Specification
Job Specification

Job Particulars

Job Title	Security Operative
Hours	Full time
Status	Permanent
Range:	Monday – Sunday (nights)

Skills and Qualities

The security operative will be:

1. Punctual and will attend work in advance of start time to be in position
2. An excellent Communicator and will have excellent verbal and written communication skills. Fluency in English is essential
3. Show exemplary personal appearance and standards
4. Capable of working on their own initiative
5. Customer focused and willing to exceed customer expectations of service
6. Discreet and capable of managing issues in a tactful and professional manner
7. Physically fit and capable for the demands of working in the security industry
8. Resilient and be able to work well under pressure

Experience and Qualifications

The ideal security operative will have:

1. A Private Security Authority licence in the door supervisor sector
2. A minimum of two years previous experience in the nightclub security industry
3. Their own transport to and from work
4. A full clean checkable work history for the past five years

164

Salary and Benefits

Rate of Pay	€16.00
Overtime	After 48 hours (based on a 6-week roster cycle)
Shift Allowance	None
Annual Leave	As per Organisation of Working Time Act 1997
Pension	Available at employee's request
Training Package	Full training package and CPD scheme
Other benefits	

Appendix 9: Security training record
Security Operative Training Record

Name:	
Date of employment:	

Initial training

Training	Date of training	Trainer
Induction		
Manual/person handling		
Crowd management		
Conflict resolution		
Physical intervention		
Fire warden		
First aid		

Refresher training

Training	Date of training	Trainer

Appendix 10 Risk assessment example
Risk Assessment

Hazard	Risk	Persons affected
Threat of violence Physical violence	Personal injury	Security staff

Risk Controls	Responsibility
Primary Controls: Security induction training Threats and violence policy and procedure Access control procedures Appropriate CCTV as deterrence to incidents	**Management:** Design of suitable polices and safe system of work procedures Organisation and supply of adequate training Supply of appropriate security uniform Supply of appropriate security equipment Supply of appropriate PPE Organisation and maintenance of correct staffing levels Supply of appropriate first aid provision and equipment Provision of post incident debriefing and organisation of appropriate post incident support (medical and psychological) Review and monitoring of incidents and identification of emerging risks. Supply and maintenance of CCTV system
Secondary controls Conflict management training Security uniform ad equipment provision to clearly identify security staff Two-way radio communications Adequate security staffing levels throughout venue Supply of appropriate PPE	
	Employees: Adherence to all company policies, procedures and safe systems of work Attend and complete required safety training Wear the supplied company uniform at all times on duty Correctly use and maintain any security equipment supplied Correctly use and maintain and PPE and first aid equipment supplied for use. Report incident of threat or physical violence to management
Tertiary Controls: Physical intervention training First aid provision Post incident debriefing Post incident support	

Recording of all incidents for review Support from Gardai and other public agencies in the event of an emergency	

Original Risk Rating		Controlled Risk Rating	
Likelihood	5	Likelihood	3
Severity	4	Severity	4
Risk Rating	20	Risk Rating	12
Recommendation	**Reduction**	Recommendation	**Accept**

Resources and Equipment		
Equipment	**PPE**	**Training**
Two-way radios CCTV Equipment Personal equipment supply	Security uniform Appropriate footwear Hi-visibility clothing Gloves	Security induction Conflict management Physical intervention First aid

Documentation and Recording		
Associated documents	**Location**	**Owner**
Access Control procedures	Control room	Head of Security
Searching procedures	Control room	Head of Security
	Control room	Head of Security
Threats and violence procedures	Control room	Head of Security
Incident reports		

Assessed by:		**Date:**	

Appendix: Acknowledgement Sheet

I hereby sign to confirm that I have received a copy of the secui
policy manual for ABC' nightclub and that I have read and under
its contents

Print Name	Signature	Date of receipt

ty

tood

Printed in Great Britain
by Amazon